International Trends in Educational Assessment

T0389723

Contemporary Approaches to Research in Learning Innovations

VOLUME 11

The titles published in this series are listed at *brill.com/carl*

International Trends in Educational Assessment

Emerging Issues and Practices

Edited by

Myint Swe Khine

BRILL

SENSE

LEIDEN | BOSTON

All chapters in this book have undergone peer review.

The Library of Congress Cataloging-in-Publication Data is available online at
http://catalog.loc.gov

ISSN 2542-8756
ISBN 978-90-04-39342-4 (paperback)
ISBN 978-90-04-39343-1 (hardback)
ISBN 978-90-04-39345-5 (e-book)

CONTENTS

PREFACE

Educational development in a country largely depends on how well progress is measured, evaluated, and assessed. An effective education system needs robust quality control and monitoring mechanisms in place to efficiently evaluate the performance of the learning organizations. In recent years, considerable attention has been given to the roles of educational measurement, evaluation, and assessment with a view to improving the education systems in general and to adequately prepare the young generation to meet the ever growing demands of the 21st century in particular.

The first International Conference on Educational Measurement, Evaluation and Assessment (ICEMEA) was organized by the Emirates College for Advanced Education (ECAE) on 5–6 November 2017 in Abu Dhabi, United Arab Emirates. The conference aimed at those working in all sectors of education and training who have a keen interest in advancing their knowledge and skills in educational measurement, evaluation, and assessment. The conference brought together eminent and distinguished speakers from Australia, France, New Zealand, Singapore, United Kingdom and United States.

The present volume comprises of selected papers from the international scholars who shared their experiences during the conference and an invited paper. Each of these chapters deals with variety of issues and practices and covers recent trends in educational assessment. The international benchmarking tests such as Programme for International Student Assessment (PISA) provides valuable information to students, teachers and policy makers on performance of the students, schools and education system. In Chapter 1, Peter Adams examined the PISA related programs and products, how the participating countries used PISA data and what is planned for PISA in the future. Zhang Quan presented an overview of Rasch model and item analysis and test equating process in for Matriculation English Test (MET) in China in Chapter 2.

In Chapter 3, Vincente Reyes from the University of Queensland, Australia and Charlene Tan from Nanyang Technological University in Singapore discuss the assessment reforms in high-performing education systems such as Shanghai and Singapore. In Chapter 4, Mark Russell and his colleagues share their experience on the Effecting Sustainable Change in Assessment Practice and Experience (ESCAPE) Project and project's sustainability and transferability.

Don Klinger from the Waikato University in New Zealand presented the pitfalls and potentials of classroom and large-scale assessments to improve educational outcome of students in Chapter 5. His presentation provided an overview of previous and ongoing research that highlights not only the necessary characteristics of large-scale assessments to inform practices and policies, but also, the skills and competencies educators require to effectively use such assessment information.

In Chapter 6, Patrick Griffin and Nafisa Awwal from the University of Melbourne, Graduate School of Education extensively described about assessment of collaborative problem-solving skills. Finally, Bahar Hasirci, Didem Karakuzular and Derin Atay pointed out the importance of assessment literacy and presented a comparative study on assessment literacy among selective Turkish teachers in Chapter 7.

I am indebted to the contributors to this volume for their time and efforts to make this book a reality. I would also like to take opportunity to thank staff members of Brill | Sense Publishers, in particular, Jasmin Lange, Chief Publishing Officer, Evelien van der Veer, Assistant Editor, and Jolanda Karada, Production Editor, for their tireless dedication in the publication process. It is hoped that this book will be a valuable resource for school administers, teachers, graduate students and researchers to keep up with the current development and trends, emerging issues and practices in educational assessment.

FIGURES AND TABLES

PETER ADAMS

1. WHAT CAN WE LEARN FROM PISA?

INTRODUCTION

The Programme for International Student Assessment, or PISA, as it is better known, has become something of an assessment phenomenon. It is global, attracts huge media attention every three years when results are released, and provokes probably more debate about 'what works' in education than any other single program or event. So, what is behind PISA's prominence and what can we learn from it? The short answer is a lot, and a lot more than is commonly understood. In this chapter I explore the well-known, as well as the much less well-known, pieces of the PISA 'enterprise'. But first, some background.

The Organisation for Economic Co-operation and Development (OECD) that is responsible for the assessment describes PISA this way:

> (PISA) is a triennial international survey which aims to evaluate education systems worldwide by testing the skills and knowledge of 15-year-old students. (http://www.oecd.org/pisa/aboutpisa/)

In 2018 approximately 540,000 students from 80 countries[1] will undertake two hours of PISA testing and another 30 minutes completing a student questionnaire. The testing assesses reading, mathematics and science because these domains[2] are regarded as foundational to a student's ongoing education. Students will also complete testing in a fourth domain that is called 'the innovative domain'. In 2015 the innovative domain was collaborative problem solving and in 2018 it is global competence.[3] Based on students' responses to the questionnaire, PISA will collect valuable information on their motivations, beliefs about themselves and their learning strategies.

Unlike most assessments, PISA is not based on a specific curriculum. Rather, it draws on content that can be found in curricula globally. Its focus is the application of knowledge and skills learned in schools to 'real life' problems that reflect what students are likely to face in life after school and at work. Therefore, the PISA assessment focuses on students' skills in analysis, reasoning and effective communication as they examine, interpret and solve problems. The emphasis is on 'literacy' rather than the recitation of specific content knowledge. In this sense, PISA is assessing how successfully students are likely to be able to apply their knowledge and skills from school to an uncertain and challenging future. The best guide to understanding what PISA is assessing, why, and how, are the assessment and analytical frameworks that are available on the PISA website.[4] These documents guide the development of the assessment and are the result of the work of a large team of international experts supported by an extensive investigation of the relevant literature. The frameworks contain key information on each domain's underpinning theory and practice, developments in thinking over time, and changing definitions and contexts. Interested readers (especially educators) who are not familiar with these frameworks are strongly encouraged to explore them to gain a rich knowledge and understanding of the foundation upon which the PISA assessment is constructed.

To take account of the breadth and diversity of the countries that participate in PISA, the OECD has put in place a complex process for ensuring that the content of the final tests and questionnaires has been evaluated against each individual country's context, especially in relation to language and culture, so that the final student performance data are valid and reliable and support robust comparisons.

PISA's prominence as the leading global assessment in education has, in part, been driven by its unique way of bringing together cognitive testing with a survey of students' attitudes and experiences – thereby enriching the analysis and reporting. While necessarily stopping short of proposing causal relationships between variables, the PISA analyses present strong correlations that are important in challenging preconceptions and assumptions, and provoking policy and reform debates.

DATA, RANKINGS AND COMPARISONS

But if PISA is well known for anything, it is for its cross-country comparisons of student performance every three years.[5] This becomes the PISA 'season' and it attracts massive international media attention and reignites global debates. Using measurement 'scales' with a distribution (or range) of PISA score points, the assessment is used to 'locate' or position each country along these scales in each domain, based on averaged student performance. This gives rise to inter-country comparisons that are often referred to in common parlance as 'league tables'. By locating countries on common scales[6] it is possible not only to examine comparative performance of countries in any one PISA assessment, but it is also possible to measure movements between countries from one assessment period to the next, and over longer periods of time.[7] Since PISA's inception, certain countries have become PISA 'success stories' and are promoted by the media and some academics and educators as models worthy of emulation. In this connection we of course think for example of Singapore, Finland, Korea, Hong Kong-China and Japan – to mention but a few. Irrespective of the merits of the case for imitation, these countries clearly have outperformed the majority of countries in some years, and for some of these countries, over repeated assessments.

However, there is an equally important metric that PISA applies to country performance that receives less public and media attention than it should, and that is the measure of equity. It is the OECD's unequivocal contention that excellence needs to be strongly complemented by equity. In PISA terms, the standout countries are those that combine high performance with a strong degree of equity. Several countries have shown that performance can be improved without being achieved at the expense of equity. From 2000 to 2012 the following countries were able to increase their performance while maintaining their levels of equity: Australia; Canada; Estonia; Finland; Hong Kong-China; Japan; Korea; Liechtenstein; Macao-China; and the Netherlands.[8]

Supporters as well as critics of PISA refer to it as a 'snapshot in time', meaning that PISA can only measure the knowledge and skills demonstrated by students at the time of the assessment. However, this should not be regarded as a criticism per se, because of course this is in fact the case for the majority of summative assessments. It is also important to note that PISA is a measure applied at the national or sub-national level,[9] not at the level of school or student. This is an important distinction between PISA and many other assessments that are designed to provide feedback at school and student level. What PISA produces is a data set of findings that show the performance of a sample of the population of 15-year-old students within the country that is scientifically representative of the population as a whole.[10] As a 'point-in-time' international assessment, PISA provides invaluable and comprehensive data on student knowledge and skills in the domains tested, and for student attitudes, experiences and motivations, and does so through an extensive series of analyses. Every three years PISA takes the educational temperature of participating countries globally.

If you were to put together a series of snapshots of your children over the years, you would see interesting changes, patterns and trends. So too with PISA. Countries that have participated in numerous cycles of PISA (some in all six cycles) can track progress over time[11] both as an absolute measure (based on average scores achieved) as well as a relative measure (based on the rank order of countries). In this way, important trends showing: improved performance; 'flat lining'; or deterioration in performance can be mapped. One such example from my own country, Australia, is the long-term decline in student performance in mathematics (2003: 525 pts, 2006: 522 pts, 2009: 515 pts, 2012: 505 pts, 2015: 494 pts).[12] The data show a steady decline of over 30 PISA score points over five consecutive PISA assessment periods. In very approximate terms, 30 PISA score points represent one year's growth in student ability. Therefore, these data show that over the period measured it can be argued that, on average, 15-year-old students in Australia have declined in their mathematics performance by the equivalent of one year of schooling. For any government this is significant and a cause for concern.

Choosing another example also from Australia, an analysis of the comparative performance of Australia's indigenous and non-indigenous students in all three domains of reading, mathematics and science provides a disturbing picture. While the trend lines over time (2000–2015)[13] in performance for each group, for each domain, remain approximately equidistant, the gap between the two sub-populations for every year, in every domain, is approximately 90 PISA score points. Using the same approximate measure of 30 score points as one year's development, these data show that Australia's first nation students are performing consistently in all domains at a level approximately three years below non-indigenous students. Again, these are data that cannot be ignored nor considered, in any sense, to be acceptable. These examples highlight how PISA data and observations should and do become central to policy and decision-making and inform education discussion and debates that need to be had within education systems globally. Many countries have made significant changes and adjustments to their education systems based on both 'snapshot' and longitudinal PISA findings.

IMPACT ON POLICY AND DECISION-MAKING

In response to PISA findings, several governments have undertaken individual country reviews. Others have: reallocated or re-prioritised resources (especially to the disadvantaged); established their own national assessment programs; complemented and validated national assessment data with PISA data; measured outcomes of their educational reforms through PISA longitudinal data; used PISA content to shape national assessment and curriculum frameworks; used PISA to guide the setting of national proficiency standards for students through a PISA-style approach; and informed policies for immigrant students. Detailed information on national responses to PISA results can be found in the work of researchers like Simon Breakspear.[14]

The 'architect' of PISA, Andreas Schleicher,[15] has persistently advocated for what he calls PISA's "myth busting" power. Using PISA findings and analyses, Schleicher reminds policy and decision makers that: top performing countries are not getting there by excluding lower performing students; 'culture' does not determine performance; if you spend more money you do not necessary improve performance; suffering deprivation does not condemn students to poor performance; it is possible to achieve excellence with a high degree of equity; the world is not divided between rich and well-educated nations and poor and badly educated ones[16]; immigrants are not depressing countries' performance; reduced class size is not a panacea for the ills of school education; and excellence does not require selectivity.[17]

EXPLORING THE DATA MORE EXTENSIVELY

While these macro policy signposts and powerful messages derived from snapshot and trend data from PISA are of real interest and importance, there is also much to be gained from taking an even closer look at the data, at the micro level. Furthermore, despite the media hype and the inordinate focus and debate generally on PISA's 'league tables' it needs to be said that among all the OECD's PISA reporting, less than 1% is constituted of comparative rankings. So, there is a great deal more to PISA, a great deal more to be explored for what it has to offer. The most comprehensive source of PISA data and information can be found in the triennial reports that are published after each PISA assessment.[18]

Volume I typically includes among its almost 500-pages data on: student performance by country in reading, mathematics and science; data on student attitudes; related socio-economic status; immigrant background; policy implications; and the relevant technical background for the volume. Volume II, with a similar page count, typically includes data and information including: policies and practices for successful schools; teaching practice; the school learning environment; school governance, assessment and accountability; selection and grouping of students; resources invested in education; policy implications of the findings; and relevant technical background.

Volume III applies a lens that typically focuses on a specific dimension of the findings in each round of PISA assessment. In 2015, for example, the PISA Results Volume III focused on student well-being. This report shines a spotlight on an increasingly crucial aspect of students' experiences at school, reflecting an important global trend in education.[19] Notably, this OECD work has brought together an authoritative combination of data, research and literature to stimulate and inform the exploration of students' experiences at school. It also investigates the impact those experiences have on our young people's success in school, and their learning more broadly.

SO, WHAT DOES THE 2015 VOLUME III TELL US?

In response to a series of questions that can be grouped under the general heading "Are students happy?", the 2015 PISA results show that on average across OECD countries, 15-year-old students are satisfied with the life they are living.[20] Regrettably, some 12% of students report not being satisfied with their life, which equates to more than 50,000 students in the global sample who are not 'happy'. Further exploring the data reveals varying levels of happiness among students across participating countries. Interestingly, high performing students do not register significantly higher levels of satisfaction. The results also confirm the phenomenon of test 'anxiety' even among those who report they feel they are well prepared. The results from the 2015 PISA student questionnaire reported in Volume III provide valuable insights into comparative levels of ambition and expectations among different countries and cohorts. There are also some indications of a weakening between 2003 and 2015 in students' sense of belonging to the school community (on average). Of concern is that one in five students reported some form of unfair treatment by their teachers (they are harshly disciplined or feel offended or ridiculed in front of others) at least a few times in each month.[21] Of even more concern are the responses from a significant percentage of students whose sense of safety and well-being at school is being violated by bullying behaviours of other students. Principals, teachers, parents and educational researchers should be stirred to thought and action in response to these findings – prompted by the dreadful consequences such behaviours can and do have on the personal well-being and academic development of these vulnerable and at-risk individuals.

Also, among the findings is an analysis of the impact on student well-being of parent engagement. Overall, there was a positive association between parent engagement and students' sense of well-being and their average performance.[22]

Parent data also shed light on the challenges and constraints they face in finding the time and opportunity to engage more with their children's school. Educators and parents alike will be interested to see the data on how long students report they spend online on a typical weekday and weekend day. Given the current uncertainty about the relative merits and disadvantages of students' online engagement, these data are timely and pertinent.

Reinforcing what many would have suspected, Volume III findings confirm the key role schools play in the development of students' social and emotional competencies. The report attests to the increased awareness of the importance of these dimensions to young peoples' lives while at the same time pointing out the lack of consensus about how best to manage for, and promote, positive outcomes for students. Student social and emotional competencies, not unexpectedly, were shown to benefit from caring and engaged teachers as well as parents.

THEMATIC REPORTS – LIGHTS UNDER A BUSHEL?

Some of the OECD's best work rarely makes it into media headlines, or unfortunately, into schools and classrooms. I refer to the OECD's PISA-based thematic reports that arise out of PISA findings. These publications draw upon the data, information, analyses, research and interpretations that are all part of the larger PISA assessment. Focusing in on aspects or dimensions of schooling, the thematic reports ultimately target improved teaching and learning. By providing breadth and depth on selected topics they can offer a more comprehensive view. A representative selection from the PISA thematic reports, for example, might include: Let's Read Them a Story! The Parent Factor in Education; Mathematics teaching and learning strategies in PISA; Problem Solving for Tomorrow's World: First Measures of Cross-Curricular Competencies from PISA; Closing the gap for immigrant students; Are students ready for a technology-rich world? What PISA studies tell us; Learners for Life: Student Approaches to Learning; Low Performing Students, Why they fall behind and how to help them succeed; and Against the Odds, Disadvantaged Students Who Succeed in School.[23]

The following excerpts from these reports are indicative of what can be found in PISA thematic reports and demonstrate why they are so valuable.

> … students show a better ability to read and learn when their parents are involved in their education and when parents themselves read. In this sense, student learning is most effective when it is the result of a partnership among the school, teachers, parents and community.[24]

> Across the group of countries studied, disciplinary climate is the teaching and learning factor that has the strongest correlation with performance … These results show that if school systems are to provide equal learning opportunities to all of their students, it is very important to improve the disciplinary climate in those schools where it is poor.[25]

Stronger problem-solving competencies and weaker mathematics performance may indicate that the mathematics instruction provided does not fully exploit the potential of students.[26]

The differences in language spoken at home and socio-economic background account for a large part of the performance gap between native and immigrant students. This indicates that immigrant students would benefit from language-centric policies and policies targeting more broadly less socio-economically advantaged students.[27]

The number of computers per student in schools has increased since PISA 2000, but it remains highly unequal across countries, and in some countries a majority of principals believe that shortage (sic) of computers is hindering instruction.[28]

… there are strong links between approaches to learning and performance in reading.[29]

… improving these other attitudes among low performers will do little to reduce students' mathematics anxiety. Instead, policy interventions to reduce mathematics anxiety could focus on improving teaching practices and classroom dynamics.[30]

This report provides a rich descriptive picture of resilience across a large number of countries. It shows that in all countries, disadvantaged students have the potential to overcome their economic and social disadvantage and to perform at levels similar to their more advantaged peers.[31]

PISA IN BRIEF – MAKING PISA 'MANAGEABLE'

The OECD has responded to the 'challenge' of PISA information and data 'overload'[32] by providing resources that are much friendlier and more immediately accessible for the busy bureaucrat, school leader or classroom teacher. These include: the PISA in Focus series[33]; the OECD's Education GPS[34]; PISA Country Notes: and the OECD Working Papers.[35]

PISA in Focus is a series of concise monthly education policy-oriented notes designed to describe a PISA topic such as: How much of a problem is bullying in schools? Do students spend enough time learning? Where did equity in education improve over the past decade? Are low performers missing learning opportunities? and Is memorisation a good strategy for learning mathematics?

The OECD's Education GPS is the OECD's source for internationally comparable data on education policies and practices, opportunities and outcomes. Accessible any time, in real time, the Education GPS provides the reader or researcher with the latest information on how countries are working to develop high-quality and equitable education systems.

Country Notes cover all the main PISA subject areas for a country, with comparative data (such as comparisons with OECD averages). Subject areas typically covered include: average performance; share of top performers; share of low performers; performance gap by gender; social equity; immigrant students; student attitudes to school and learning; and student well-being.[36]

Finally, another valuable resource for educators is the OECD's series of Education Working Papers. This series goes well beyond PISA-related topics and as such is an invaluable asset for educators and researchers. However, those interested in PISA-related research need only search the database to find topics such as: A Framework for the Analysis of Student Well-Being in the PISA 2015 Study: Being 15 In 2015; Comparison of PIAAC and PISA Frameworks for Numeracy and Mathematical Literacy; PISA in Low and Middle-Income Countries and The Policy Impact of PISA: An Exploration of the Normative Effects of International Benchmarking in School System Performance.

PISA DERIVATIVES

The positive and powerful impact of PISA has given rise to a number of projects and initiatives that I have called PISA 'derivatives'.

The most significant program to be developed from the global PISA assessment is the OECD's PISA-based Test for Schools ('PISA for Schools'). PISA for Schools is a student assessment tool, used by schools to support research, benchmarking and school improvement. It provides descriptive information and analyses on the skills and creative application of knowledge of 15-year-old students in reading, mathematics, and science comparable to main PISA scales. It also provides information on how factors within and outside of school are linked to student performance. Student questionnaires are an important part of the assessment, collecting information on socio-economic background, attitudes and interests in reading, science and mathematics, and the school learning environment.[37]

So, what is the relationship between PISA for Schools and the international PISA main study?

While the international PISA assessment is designed to produce national results that can be used for international comparisons and to inform policy discussions, PISA for Schools is designed to provide school-level results for benchmarking and school-improvement purposes. Therefore, PISA for Schools is not intended for ranking school performance which is likely to work against inter-school collaboration and school improvement. Rather, it is designed for making appropriate and helpful comparisons. The PISA for Schools test items have been developed using the same assessment frameworks as the main PISA studies and imitate their design and style, but the items themselves are different. The school results based on the students' performance[38] in the test are analysed by the OECD using a methodology that generates scores on the 'PISA scale'. These scores are therefore comparable to PISA scores and can be used to make valid comparisons with PISA performance.

A school's results can be used for different comparisons. Firstly, schools can use their data within peer learning situations, such as within communities of professional practice where principals and staff can work together using a base of comparable data from the tests. For example, students at School A may perform highly on mathematics, but less well on reading. School B on the other hand may experience the reverse – high reading performance but lower performance in mathematics. By collaborating and sharing ideas and practice these two schools stand a very good chance of learning how they might improve in their specific areas of lesser performance. In a similar way, some school districts (especially in the United States) have used the tests to form a baseline for comparison between schools within a district. Once again, the comparisons make sense to all the schools involved because they have data that is directly comparable. Networks of collaboration and peer learning are very active within US districts that are participating in the program.

An additional value provided by the PISA scores from this program are that schools and groups of schools can be compared to other countries that have participated in PISA. Schools, groups of schools, or even school systems who undertake PISA for Schools can nominate a suitable selection of countries against whom they wish to be compared. Such 'international benchmarking' has proved particularly popular among program participants. Furthermore, this has in a sense, gone some way to bridging the gap between the national relevance of PISA and its value in schools and classrooms.

The extensive report generated by the program for participating schools contains not only the school's data, but also international benchmarking and case studies together with guides on observed effective practice drawing from examples internationally.[39] The PISA for Schools program is growing in popularity globally and at the time of writing included, among others, the following participating countries[40]: Spain; United States; Russian Federation; United Kingdom; Brunei, United Arab Emirates; Brazil, Mexico and Colombia.

A SECOND OUTGROWTH FROM PISA OCCURRED IN 2016–2017

Working in consultation with the OECD, the PISA4U[41] pilot project was developed and delivered by Candena[42] using a unique online learning delivery platform, supported by donor funding.[43] While having 'pilot' status in its first iteration, the project's success is likely to encourage subsequent iterations of the project.[44] PISA4U works as an online programme for school improvement. Using a unique collaborative online programme PISA4U brings together educational practitioners who can learn from one another, drive improvement in schools distributed around the world, and create an international database of teaching resources that will be accessible to educators worldwide.

Based on a collaborative eDidactic format, participants[45] work in teams on a series of successive assignments that guide them towards designing new educational resources and solutions that address their immediate needs. They benefit from learning resources from experts in education and best practices from international school case studies, as well as mentorship and peer feedback throughout the programme. The focus of the programme is to build a global network of educators that will act as a driving force for making a meaningful contribution to school improvement. Participants in the program become part of a small team of motivated and engaged educators. Team members move through a series of assignments and develop innovative solutions that can be implemented in school environments (including their own).

Members have special access to quality insights from international experts in education, as well as the expertise and best practices of pioneering educational institutions from Singapore, Malta, Arizona, and Israel. Throughout the programme, each team is assisted by a dedicated mentor, who acts as a trusted guide and point of contact for help. Each team is required to complete 5 assignments. The platform facilitates virtual meetings and the exchange of ideas and information between members of the team. It showcases how international collaboration is feasible and effective.

The PISA4U pilot project attracted 4,700 registrants from 172 countries. Among the participants were 3,864 teachers, 383 school administrators, 174 trainee teachers, 90 government officials, 49 students, 43 parents, with the remainder being 'interested parties'. Participants ranged in age from 13 to 80 years. The ten countries with the greatest number of participants were (in order): Romania; United States; Philippines; India; Pakistan; Nigeria; Mexico, Brazil, Italy; and Colombia. The pilot project continued for a period of 15 weeks. Overall, the teams produced well over 100 resources that responded to specific problems posed to them during the project.

A Paris-based event at the OECD to showcase some of the high-quality resources produced clearly demonstrated the potential and efficacy of strong collaboration between team members. Of particular interest was the fact that despite the diversity of backgrounds, nationalities, geographic locations and ages of participants, as a group, they were still able to agree on the top five 'challenges' facing teachers and schools today. They included in order of priority: motivating students; classroom management and disciplinary issues; parental involvement; fostering 21st century skills in the classroom; and the use of technology in education.

CONCLUDING REMARKS

Is There an Ongoing Role for PISA? Clearly, the Answer Is Yes

Firstly, PISA remains the pre-eminent international assessment testing the performance of education systems globally, focussing on students' cognitive skills and abilities, their attitudes, values and experiences, comparative levels of equity, and increasingly, student well-being. Undoubtedly PISA serves what is a growing need globally. 72 countries participated in PISA 2015, 80 will participate in PISA 2018 and it is estimated that potentially more than 100 countries could be included in PISA 2021. Clearly its importance and relevance are growing, not declining.

Secondly, PISA data permeates education decision making, research, literature, debates and planning world-wide. It is hard to conceive of any international education space that is not linked in some way to the work of PISA. Finally, it must be emphasised that PISA is owned and funded by 35 OECD member countries together with participating countries and economies – that is, 80 countries/economies in total. Its custodian is the OECD, but it is an international asset. This is something often lost in the debates about PISA. The program was designed and developed to respond to a need among countries for an accurate, reliable and robust global measure of educational performance in the foundational areas of reading, mathematics and science. Over its eighteen-year history, PISA has been through a series of enhancements, expansions and has responded to changing contexts and expectations.

PISA is in no sense an 'imposition' on the world's education systems, quite to the contrary, it is a response to their clearly expressed needs.

NOTES

[1] A list of countries participating in the 2018 PISA assessment can be found at: http://www.oecd.org/pisa/contacts/pisagoverningboard.htm

[2] A list of countries participating in the 2018 PISA assessment can be found at: http://www.oecd.org/pisa/contacts/pisagoverningboard.htm

[3] For a discussion of the innovative domain refer: https://www.tes.com/news/school-news/breaking-views/if-soft-skills-really-matter-then-we-should-try-measure-them

[4] http://www.oecd.org/pisa/data/

[5] The latest such 'release' of PISA findings was for the 2015 PISA assessment, published in December 2016.

[6] One for each of the domains assessed.

[7] 'Longitudinal' data that typically spans many PISA assessments, which for some countries is from 2000 to 2015.

[8] http://www.keepeek.com/Digital-Asset-Management/oecd/education/pisa-2012-results-excellence-through-equity-volume-ii_9789264201132-en#.WoUrbqiWZPY#, page 13.

[9] Countries have the option to 'over-sample' the national student population to enable PISA reporting at a sub-national geographic region (for example, at the level of a state or province).

[10] Some degree of confusion and misunderstanding exists publicly about the use of sampling and the extent of its accuracy. The PISA assessment employs technically robust, scientific and accurate sampling, reinforcing the reliability of its findings. For detailed technical information on PISA sampling refer: http://www.oecd.org/pisa/sitedocument/PISA-2015-Technical-Report-Chapter-4-Sample-Design.pdf

[11] Based on 'longitudinal' data (tracking data at different points in time).

[12] Approximate figures for purposes of the example.

[13] The trends informing this example are derived from the following PISA assessment years: reading 2000–2015, mathematics 2003–2015, and science literacy 2006–2015.

[14] Refer for example to: www.oecd.org/officialdocuments/publicdisplaydocumentpdf/ and http://simonbreakspear.com/wp-content/uploads/2015/09/Breakspear-PISA-Paper.pdf

[15] Andreas Schleicher is the Director for Education and Skills, and Special Advisor on Education Policy to the Secretary-General at the OECD, Paris.

[16] Less than a quarter of the performance variation among OECD countries can be explained by GDP per capita (and this rises to 36% among all participating countries).

[17] https://all4ed.org/debunking-seven-myths-about-pisa/

[18] Typically, the PISA Results Volumes I and II are published toward the end of the next year after the assessment (for example, PISA 2015 results were published in December 2016).

[19] Over recent years there has been a proliferation of research, literature, surveys and programs in schools focussing on student well-being.

[20] http://www.oecd-ilibrary.org/docserver/download/3512d7ae- en.pdf?expires=1518599823&id=id&a ccname=guest&checksum=16CAEE56D74746B5127565F49D1185D1

[21] Ibid.

[22] Student performance as measured in 2015 by their results in the major domain of science.

[23] These are many other titles can be accessed at: http://www.oecd-ilibrary.org/education/pisa_19963777

[24] http://www.keepeek.com/Digital-Asset-Management/oecd/education/let-s-read-them-a-story-the-parent-factor-in-education_9789264176232-en#.WoV81YVOJPY#, page 13.

[25] http://www.keepeek.com/Digital-Asset-Management/oecd/education/mathematics-teaching-and-learning-strategies-in-pisa_9789264039520-en#, page 146.

[26] http://www.keepeek.com/Digital-Asset-Management/oecd/education/problem-solving-for-tomorrow-s-world_9789264006430-en#, page 55.

[27] http://www.keepeek.com/Digital-Asset-Management/oecd/education/closing-the-gap-for-immigrant-students_9789264075788-en#.WoW2mYVOJPY#, page 9.

[28] http://www.keepeek.com/Digital-Asset-Management/oecd/education/are-students-ready-for-a-technology-rich-world_9789264036093-en#.WoW31oVOJPY#, page 16.

[29] http://www.keepeek.com/Digital-Asset-Management/oecd/education/are-students-ready-for-a-technology-rich-world_9789264036093-en#.WoW31oVOJPY#, page 16.

[30] http://www.keepeek.com/Digital-Asset-Management/oecd/education/low-performing-students_9789264250246-en#, page 122.

[31] http://www.keepeek.com/Digital-Asset-Management/oecd/education/against-the-odds_9789264090873-en#, page 82.

[32] Noting that as previously explained, some of the 2015 PISA reports are each nearly 500 pages in length.

[33] http://www.oecd.org/pisa/pisaproducts/pisainfocus.htm

[34] http://gpseducation.oecd.org/

[35] http://www.oecd-ilibrary.org/education/oecd-education-working-papers_19939019

[36] For an example of a Country Note visit https://www.oecd.org/pisa/PISA-2015-United-States.pdf

[37] http://www.oecd.org/pisa/aboutpisa/pisa-based-test-for-schools.htm

[38] The test is completed by a school sample of between 35 and 80 students. It is not appropriate to test a sample smaller than 35 students in a school because the resulting data and findings will not be technically robust and reliable.

[39] An example of the PISA-based Test for Schools school report can be found at: http://www.oecd.org/pisa/aboutpisa/Golden_e-book_1_example.pdf

[40] Included in this list are countries that have completed the program or are undertaking it currently.

[41] https://www.pisa4u.org/

[42] CANDENA is a learning technologies company founded to enable organizations to reach global audiences and engage them with inspiring educational offerings. It is an offshoot from Lüneburg's Leuphana University in Northern Germany and has been created as part of the University's EU Innovation Incubator. More information on the organisation is available at www.candena.com

[43] The pilot was made possible through the generous support of America Achieves and Deutsche Telekom Stiftung. The program was conceptually designed, implemented and administered by CANDENA GmbH.

[44] The pilot was made possible through the generous support of America Achieves and Deutsche Telekom Stiftung. The program was conceptually designed, implemented and administered by CANDENA GmbH.

[45] In the pilot project, participants were educational practitioners including teachers, administrators, education policy actors, and educational researchers, globally.

Peter Adams
Ministry of Education
Kingdom of Saudi Arabia

ZHANG QUAN

2. RASCH MODEL

Research and Practice in China

INTRODUCTION

This chapter is organized into three parts. The first part presents an overview of Rasch Model: status quo in China with a focus on item analysis and Matriculation English Test (MET) test equating project during 1990–1999. The second part gives a brief introduction to Pacific-Rim Objective Measurement Symposium (PROMS) conference, and translation work on Rasch measurement since PROMS2012 was held in China; the third part will briefly discuss the Rasch prospect, significance, and limitations in China. The purpose of this chapter is to share experience, exchange ideas and learn from each other. It was found that Rasch-based research work is increasingly taking place in Mainland China with promising signs and prospects.

RASCH MODEL AND TEST EQUATING FOR MET IN CHINA

As early as in the 1980s, the ideas and concepts regarding the Rasch Model and IRT were first introduced into China by Professor Gui Shichun, my Ph.D. supervisor, and it is Professor Gui who first used Rasch Model to conduct with great success the ten-year-long (1990–1999) Equating Project for Matriculation English Test (MET) in China. MET is the most influential and competitive entrance examination for higher education, administered annually by Examination Authority under Ministry of Education of the Chinese government. In 1978, over 3.3 million candidates took up the exam, and the number is increasing every year. At the present time, the number swells to approximately 10 million candidates. The equating practice won recognition by Charles Alderson, Lyle F. Bachman, and other foreign counterparts during the 1990s. Academically, those were Good Old Days for Chinese testing experts and psychometricians. Then for certain reasons, the equating practice abruptly discontinued. Therefore, in China nowadays, the application of Rasch Model or the IRT-based software like BILOG, PARSCA, Winsteps, GITEST and others to real testing problem solving is confined within a small group of people.

Features of the MET

The MET is the most influential and competitive entrance examination for higher education across Mainland China, centrally organized by Examination Authority under the Ministry of Education of the Chinese government. The MET can be listed at least in the following five aspects: compulsory, large-scale yet high stake, administered at the national level, mainly multiple choice questions together with a small portion of writing and test equating via anchored items that have been in practice annually from 1990–1999.

Compulsory. The MET is compulsory because all the Chinese middle school students must take the test if they are planning to study in a college or a university after graduation from middle schools.

Large-scale yet high-stake. The MET is a large-scale high stake entrance examination. The number of candidates was over 3.3 million in 1978 and reached approximately 10 million in recent years. The pass or fail largely decides the rest of test takers' career life; therefore, schools, parents and families in China pay great attention to the test. Though some reforms are carried out since 2016, for example, students may be given two attempts to take the test and choose the higher scores for university admission, it is still of a high-stake in nature. If the 'higher' score of the two attempts out to be below the passing score set by the examination authority, the student cannot be admitted.

Administered at the national level. The MET is paper-based, centrally organized by Examination Authority under Ministry of Education of the Chinese government. The same MET paper is used at the given time across China.

Mainly multiple-choice questions plus a small portion of the writing. The MET paper consists of multiple-choice questions together with a small portion of writing. The multiple choice question parts fall into four categories: phonetics, grammar, fill-in-the-blank, and reading comprehension, which amount to 85% of the test. The essay writing on a given topic carries 15%.

Implementation of test equating via anchored items. The MET test equating via anchored items was conducted from 1990–1999. Test scores, after conversion, can be comparable on the same scale to ensure test fairness for all the test takers each time the MET is administered. The author comes to realize that such a project reflects the most evident Chinese characteristics because not all the countries need such a test equating. The unique situation has been described by Gui Shichun (1990) and Gui Shichun, Li Wei, and Zhang Quan (1993). This is a ten-year test equating project of the MET sponsored by the Examination Authority under the Ministry of Education of China.

In the first place, due to the uneven development of education and the big number of candidates taking the test, the population is no longer homogenous even though candidates are all senior middle school graduates. From the viewpoint of language testing, it would be difficult to set an unbiased test, let alone to equate two parallel test forms administered on different occasions. Next, although the test papers were centrally produced in Beijing, there was no way yet to score the papers centrally. The general practice was/is to assign every individual province to grade its papers and to work out its norm for recruitment. The university authorities face the problem of selecting candidates whose scores were graded according to different criteria set up by different provincial testing departments. Apart from this, in China, there is no feasible way to protect test security immediately after its administration. Nor is it possible to use common items in different forms, nor is feasible to conduct any pre-test for future use.

OUR HYPOTHESIS

There will be no big changes regarding general means (English proficiency) within one year's time. If there is any change of means, it must be associated with the change of difficulty level of test forms across two years (Gui Shichun, Li Wei, & Zhang Quan, 1993).

Anchor-Test-Random-Groups Design

To find a feasible solution(s) to such problems, we established an anchorage, i.e., three sampling bases (middle schools) to monitor the performance of the candidates. We designed an equivalent test form (35+65=100 items) and had it administered to the candidates who were going to take the MET three days before the MET was administered. The equivalent test form was used repeatedly for ten years (1990–1999). In doing so, we could not only observe but also compare the performance of candidates taking the MET in different years (Gui Shichun, Li Wei, & Zhang Quan, 1993). The concept of 'equating' discussed here refers to linking of test forms through common items so that scores derived from the tests which were administered separately to different test takers on different occasions after conversion will be comparable on the same scale (Hambleton & Swaminathan et al., 1985). The idea regarding Anchor-test-random-groups design is illustrated in Figure 2.1. The equivalent test was taken externally, three days before the MET was administered. For ten years running (1990–1999), the author of the present paper collected the data in the designated sampling school and used GITEST, BILOG, and PARSCALE to calibrate the test items and compared the equated parameters during his Ph.D. studies.

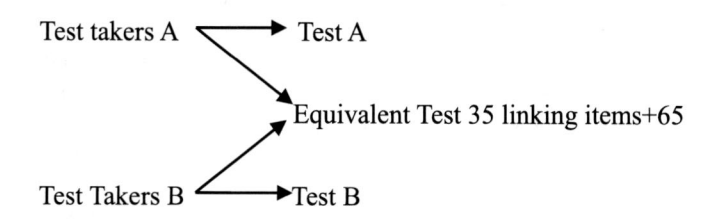

Figure 2.1. The idea regarding anchor-test-random-groups design

The Anchor-test-random-groups design is implemented in the phases summarized as follows.

The first phase is sampling. Sampling refers to data collecting via an equivalent test in the designated sampling schools. The test results of the MET88 (the year when MET was first administered across China) was used as a basal reference. Chi-square test (Wright, 1979) of the 35 linking items was applied to delete the inappropriate items. In 1989, we used 28 items; in 1990–1991, we had 27 items. In what follows, with anchor test, via Rasch Model, we used GITEST, our Rasch-based program developed by ourselves, all the following test forms were equated (calibrated and rescaled) (Wright, 1979).

Ability Estimation

In the case of the Rasch Model, the ability estimation is straightforward. To obtain the maximum likelihood estimation of theta (θ), we used the Newton-Raphson procedure (Hambleton, 1985). The ability values are again converted into probabilities for those who know nothing about Rasch within the education sector in China. As the model has the sample-free feature, we could make use of the derived data to obtain adjusted scores for the population.

Why Rasch Model?

Rasch model is a simple yet old model for conducting assessment research. More than half a century has passed since the Danish mathematician Georg Rasch (1901–1981) published his "Probabilistic Model for Intelligence and Attainment Tests" (Rasch, 1960). With this departure, the model has been applied in measuring variables ranging from psychology, medicine, management, teaching, and testing and extended from the initial application to the dichotomous data type to the polytomous data. Today, the model is known as "Rasch Model" among measurement professionals and testing practitioners who have a vision of promoting objective measurement.

In the author's opinion, of all the objective measurement approaches that are at the disposal of researchers and practitioners over the past century, the Rasch model is the most versatile, powerful and feasible. Its versatility comes from the way in which it enjoys increasingly applied to a wider range of research fields ranging from the social, behavioral and health science, a means, for instance, in performing item analysis, test scoring and equating in language testing.

The power of Rasch derives from the way in which it enables the researchers and practitioners to construct variables to produce objective measurement or to provide an adequate explanation for the solution of their problems. The feasibility of Rasch lies in that data matrix either dichotomous or polytomous can be processed using the Rasch-based software. With a single click of a mouse, all the results would be saved in the designated file for further use. It is in the sense that the Rasch model meets the requirements of the MET in China. Once the item parameters were calibrated, the corresponding ability parameters can be estimated. The other reason is model-data

Table 2.1. Item difficulty of MET 1988–1992

	MET88	MET89	MET90	MET91	MET92
Phonetics	−0.860 (.70)	−0.69(0.48)	0.793 (0.31)	−0.186 (0.55)	0.992 (0.28)
Grammar	0.228 (.44)	−0.372(0.59)	0.471 (0.38)	0.500 (0.38)	0.801 (0.31)
BLK-Filling	−0.367 (.59)	0.271(0.43)	0.871 (0.30)	0.845 (0.30)	0.609 (0.35)
Reading	−0.330(.58)	−0.581(0.64)	0.600 (0.35)	−0.179 (0.54)	−0.202 (0.55)
Means	−0.206 (.55)	−0.180(0.54)	0.657 (0.34)	0.361 (0.41)	0.523 (0.37)

Table 2.2. Ability (θ) of MET 1988–1992

	MET88	MET89	MET90	MET91	MET92
Total N	136543	117085	128543	136047	133965
θ Means	40.0	44.4	53.7	50.0	54.2
%	47.0	52.2	63.2	58.8	63.8
SD	17.9	16.1	13.5	missing	15.2

fit. With the Rasch model, item and ability fit can be computed (Wright, 1982) and we can demonstrate the degree of goodness-of-fit of the model.

For better illustration, the numbers in brackets are probabilities converted from difficulties. As shown in Table 2.1, no big differences between MET88 and MET89; however, MET90 turned out to be more difficult.

The θ means as shown in Table 2.2 refer to the rescaled average ability parameters 40.0 regarding the multiple choice (MC) parts only, the full score is 85; 85 MC + 15 Writing = 100.

GITEST Program

The GITEST program we used is a Rasch-based program developed by a Ph.D. program of applied linguistics headed by Prof. Gui Shichun of Guangzhou Institute of Foreign Languages, China in 1983. It was written in BASIC according to Rasch Model which is good at performing the following functions:

- It assumes binary (right-wrong) scoring;
- Designed for applications of both CTT and Rasch to practical testing problems;
- Maximum likelihood (ML);
- Tests of fit for individual items;
- Analysis of multiple subtests in one pass;
- Item analysis and test paper evaluation and report;
- Feedback for teaching and testing improvement;
- Linking of 2 test forms through common items;
- 200 items/10,000 candidates/in a single run;

The statistics used by GITEST is listed below:

Mean	the mean scores of the whole examinees;
SD	the standard deviations of the whole examinees;
Varn.	the variants based on the whole examinees;
P+	probability of correct answers;
Pd	Δ value, difficulty parameter based on probability;
R11	by Kuder-Richardson 20, reliability, this value should be over 0.9
aVALUE	reliability parameter, also called α value, by Cronbach formula, this value should be over 0.8
Rbis	discrimination index (in the unit of bi-serial)
Skewness	score distribution value
	0 indicating normal distribution;
	above 0, indicating positive skewness, showing the test items more difficulty;
	below 0, indicating negative skewness, showing the test items easier;
Kurtosis	score distribution height:
	0 indicating normal; above 0 showing "narrower", i.e. small range between the scores; below 0, indicating "flat", i.e. big range between scores;
Difficulty VD	(<0.1), D(=0.1~0.3), I(0.3~0.7), E(0.7~0.9), VE(>0.9)

GITEST, BILOG and PARSCALE Compared

To justify the parameters yielded by our GITEST, we used GITEST, BILOG, and PARSCALE to process the same group of data. Figure 2.2 shows the three curves generated by GITST, BILOG, and PARSCALE, indicating item difficulties based on the same data (1990–1999).

As shown in Figure 2.2, the curves are very close. The BILOG and PARSCALE are almost overlapping. This is due to the number of cycles and the pre-determined value for convergence set in a respective command file. BILOG came to convergence

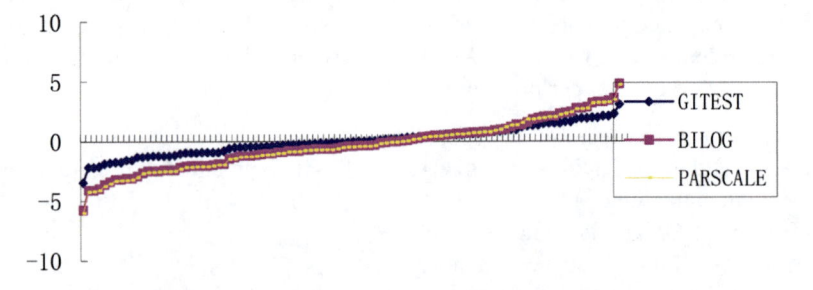

Figure 2.2. Three curves generated by GITEST, BILOG, and PARSCALE

after six cycles with the largest changes = 0.005, while PARSCALE came to convergence after 72 cycles with the LARGEST CHANGE = 0.01. GITEST looks a little bit different. This is because all the parameters are set as defaults. On the whole, there is almost no difference regarding test item difficulty calibration of these three computer programs.

GITEST and WINSTEPS Compared

To further justify the parameters yielded by GITEST, we used GITEST and WINSTEPS to process the same group of data. Figure 2.3 shows the curves generated by GITEST and WINSTEPS, indicating item difficulties based on the same data.

Figure 2.3 shows item difficulties of Test A and Test B obtained from GITEST and WINSTEPS. The two curves of each test look almost overlapping. This has been further confirmed that GITEST we developed works as well as the other Rasch-based programs.

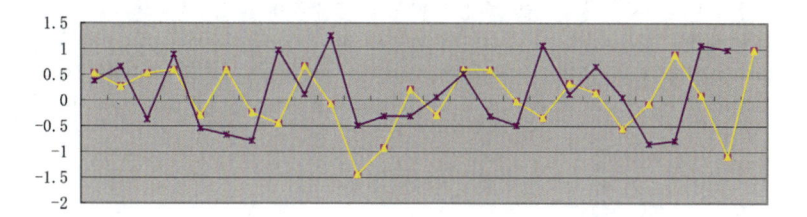

Figure 2.3. Four curves generated by GITEST and WINSTEPS

PROMS IN CHINA

The PROMS, abbreviated from Pacific-Rim Objective Measurement Symposium, is an international research society established to promote objective measurement and contribute to the research and development of Rasch measurement in the Pacific Rim countries and regions. Since 2005, PROMS conference is held each year in one of these countries and regions to provide a forum for the sharing of new knowledge with the international community. Pre-conference workshops focusing on Rasch measurement are usually attached to PROMS meetings. Each time experts of Rasch are invited to offer the practice of Rasch measurement, to show how to use WINSTEPS to young teachers, researchers and Ph.D. students coming from Pacific-rim regions and countries and beyond. The principal aims of PROMS are to:

1. Encourage the pursuit of Rasch measurement in the Pacific region and its application in the fields of Business, Counseling, Economics, Education, Health Care, Language, Measurement, Psychology, Quality Assurance, Statistics, and Strategic Planning;

2. Advocate measurement practice that contributes to individual, community and societal well-being, and the public good, in the Pacific region;
3. Raise the visibility and status of Rasch measurement in the Pacific region (Cavanagh & Fisher, 2014).

These aims are to be accomplished through:

1. Establishing a Pacific region network of researchers and scholars to foster cooperative and collaborative relationships;
2. Holding an annual meeting—the Pacific Rim Objective Measurement Symposium;
3. Providing workshops and training;
4. Engaging in such other activities as might facilitate the development of research, policy, and practice in Rasch measurement (Cavanagh & Fisher, 2014).

In particular, the author wishes to highlight that it was Professor Magdalena Mo Ching Mok of the Education University of Hong Kong who introduced PROMS into both Mainland China and Taiwan. The first PROMS conference was held in Jiaxing in 2012, and the following one was in Kaohsiung in 2013. PROMS2014 was in Guangzhou, PROMS2016 in Xi'an and PROMS2018 in Shanghai. Due to these regular conferences and exposure, Rasch-based research projects and translation of Rasch measurement literature are gaining momentum in China in recent years.

Research Project

Among many Rasch-based research projects, the one worth mentioning is the project recently conducted *ad hoc* for comparison of English listening and reading comprehension between two important English language tests: General English Proficiency Test (GEPT) in Taiwan and College English Test (CET) in Mainland China (Quang Zhang et al., 2014; Hong Yang & Mingzhu Miao, 2015).

Test Descriptions

General English Proficiency Test (GEPT) in Taiwan is a test of English proficiency with five levels currently being administered: elementary, intermediate, high-intermediate, advanced and quality, of which the High-Intermediate level is administered ad hoc for university students of non-English majors.

College English Test Band 4 (CET-4) is a test of English proficiency for the educational purpose designed by Shanghai Jiaotong University according to the requirements of college English teaching and administered to sophomore students of non-English majors only. The CET has been administered ever since 1987 across Mainland China and even beyond. The number of CET test takers remains the highest in the world.

Research Purpose

An online search shows that no significant research has been conducted to compare GEPT and CET so far. PROMS2013 held in Kaohsiung sparked the action and made such research feasible. Also, the time has been matured to make such a comparison with focus on both test takers' ability and test item difficulty regarding listening and reading comprehension in the Chinese context. Rasch model turns out to be the most appropriate measurement to fulfill the task.

Significances and Limitations

The research project, while focusing on the comparison of GEPT and CET, presents the research method via Rasch supported with real data analyses and thus can be concluded in two points as follows.

This is a pioneering attempt conducted in language testing field across Taiwan Strait. The most significant parts of the research are listed below:

1. To show to our teachers of English, the importance of item analysis and test scoring with the help of Rasch-based computer software;
2. To demonstrate how item analysis and test scoring are conducted using GITEST (Rasch-based computer software) and
3. How to understand the ideas regarding the Rasch Model with detailed inter-pretation.

However, two limitations exist – small sample size and further justification are needed to administer the same test items to the students with a homogenous background in Taiwan in the same manner.

Translation Work

The Rasch model is known to be the most versatile, powerful and practical. However, descriptions of such versatile, powerful and practical approaches are mostly written in the English language. The understanding, dissemination, and flexibility of the model are never fully experienced by a majority of Chinese speaking researchers. This situation existed in the academic circle for a long time. Motivated by this, the editors first met in 2013 to discuss the possibility of publishing translation, with permission by Dr. Richard M. Smith, into both simplified and traditional Chinese, the English abstracts related to Rasch-based research from the Journal of Applied Measurement (JAM), a scholarly peer-reviewed journal of measurement applications with an emphasis on the family of Rasch measurement models. The goal was to produce books that would give readers in Chinese-speaking countries general research information regarding Rasch measurement conducted in other parts of the world.

JAM Book of Abstract Translation

The Constructing Variables and JAM Book of Abstracts (Vols. I and II) were translated from English to Chinese and published in the past two years. These two volumes contain 410 abstracts from JAM germane to Rasch-based research work translated from English into both Simple and Classic Chinese by 45 highly competent translators who are working in 13 different organizations, universities or institutes located respectively in China Mainland, Hong Kong, Macau, and Taiwan.

Each of these abstracts deals with Rasch measures in their research field, covering a variety of issues ranging from education, psychology, management, testing to medicine. The abstracts also serve as valuable resources for researchers and students of non-English majors in Mainland China and Chinese-speaking researchers to be able to conduct their Rasch model analyses as well as understand and critique Rasch-based research publications.

JAM Book of Full Paper Translation

Even though the abstract books are published, the author/editors realize that the versatile, powerful and practical approaches of Rasch are still far from being widely understood or used outside a relatively small group of *Raschers*. Full paper translation is needed to meet such the situation in China. From the beginning of 2017, the team prepared to systematic translation of the representative papers from the Understanding Rasch Measurement Series in the JAM. The translators put their relentless efforts in making sure that the original concepts, issues, and examples presented to help explain various principles and applications in Rasch are reflected in the translated versions. In 2018, at Technology-Enhanced Assessment Conference in Hong Kong was launched a ceremony for a new book of full paper translation entitled Introduction to Rasch Measurement in traditional Chinese and Simplified Chinese version.

The full paper translation contains 24 chapters deliberately selected from the previously published *Journal of Applied Measurement*, under the Understanding Rasch Measurement series and addresses three major areas: Theory, Models, and Applications. All the authors are the experienced *Raschers*. Dr. Richard M. Smith stated in the Theory section contains the basics of Rasch measurement and how Rasch measurement differs from item response theory (IRT). The chapter by Wright and Mok presents the Rasch models commonly used in the social and health sciences.

The two chapters by Linacre discuss estimation methods for these models. Estimation of model parameters is logically followed by a discussion of the assessment of the fit data to a model in a chapter by R. Smith. E. Smith then presents an overview of how the traditional conceptualizations of reliability and validity can be addressed in the context of Rasch measurement. Finally, the chapters by Wilson and Andrich discuss the underlying philosophy and rationale of Rasch measurement and why some researchers prefer to use Rasch models rather than IRT models. In reality, each chapter is very informative and some, if expanded, would be important topics not only for newcomers but also for postgraduate students.

Monograph Translation

Thus far the translation from English into Chinese of the monograph *Applying the Rasch Model: Fundamental Measurement in the Human Sciences* by Professor Trevor Bond and Christine M. Fox has been completed and ready to be published. It took more than six years to prepare the book. The book contains all the chapters germane to Rasch theory and ideas by eight highly competent translators working in 5 different organizations, universities or institutes located throughout Mainland China and Hong Kong. The translation serves in particular as an invaluable resource for researchers and students in China Mainland to be able to learn and to self-teach Rasch and conduct their Rasch-based analyses as well as understand and critique Rasch-based research publications. Though highly theoretic, the book can be used as a textbook for postgraduate students of applied linguistics in the Chinese-speaking community as well.

The past three years witness such published translation works proven to be valuable resources for the Rasch community of Chinese-speaking researchers and practitioners who were interested in gaining a better perspective of how Rasch models are used for and why it is also called One-Parameter Model. The author is confident that the translation of abstract books together with full paper translation chapters cover almost all the topics for Rasch measurement. Anyone who is seriously interested in research and development in the field of Rasch family will find the books to be an excellent source of information and guideline regarding application of the Rasch model.

RASCH MODEL: FUTURE IN CHINA

The Rasch-based research is increasing in China. More young researchers have come to realize the importance and usefulness of Rasch measurement. The progress made so far to introduce Rasch is encouraging. For all *Raschers*, rigorous measurement has been essential to the advancement of civilization since Babylonian times, and to the advancement of physical science since the Renaissance and will certainly keep the measurement approaches with the rhythm of computer and Internet era.

REFERENCES

Cavanagh, R. F., & Fisher, W. (2015). Be wary of what's coming from the West: Globalisation and the implications for measurement in the human sciences. In Q. Zhang & H. Yang (Eds.), *Pacific Rim Objective Measurement Symposium (PROMS) 2014 Conference Proceedings*. Berlin & Heidelberg: Springer.

Gui Shichun. (1990). *Construction of item bank* (Selected Academic Works by Examination Authority under Ministry of Education of China). Beijing: Guangming Daily Press.

Gui Shichun, Li Wei, & Zhang Quan. (1993). *An application IRT to test equating of MET in China* (Selected Academic Works by Examination Authority under Ministry of Education of China). Beijing: Peace Press.

Hambleton, R. K., & Swaminathan, H. (1985). *Item response theory: Principles and applications.* Boston, MA: Kluwer Academic Publishers.

Mok, M., & Zhang, Q. (Ed.). (2014). *Constructing variables: Book of abstracts* (Vol. I). Maple Grove, MN: JAM Press.

Mok, M., & Zhang, Q. (Ed.). (2015). *Constructing variables: Book of abstracts* (Vol. II). Maple Grove, MN: JAM Press.

Mok, M., & Zhang, Q. (Ed.). (2018). *Translation of introduction to Rasch measurement.* Maple Grove, MN: JAM Press.

Wright, B. D., Mead, X. J., & Bell, S. (1982). *BICAL: Calibrating items with the Rasch model. Research memorandum 23C.* Chicago, IL: University of Chicago, Department of Education.

Wright, B. D., & Stone, M. H. (1979). *Best test design: Rasch measurement.* Chicago, IL: MESA.

Yang Hong, & Mingzhu Miao. (2015). *A Rasch-based approach for comparison of English reading comprehension between CET and GEPT.* (PROMS) 2014 Conference Proceedings, Berlin & Heidelberg: Springer.

Zhang Quan, Guoxiong He, & Huifeng Mu. (2015). A Rasch-based approach for comparison of English listening comprehension between CET and GEPT. In Quan Zhang & Hong Yang (Eds.), *Pacific Rim Objective Measurement Symposium (PROMS) 2014 Conference Proceedings.* Berlin & Heidelberg: Springer.

Zhang Quan
Institute of Language Testing and College of Foreign Studies
University of Jiaxing
Zhejiang, P.R. China

VICENTE REYES AND CHARLENE TAN

3. ASSESSMENT REFORMS IN HIGH-PERFORMING EDUCATION SYSTEMS

Shanghai and Singapore

INTRODUCTION

Shanghai and Singapore are widely regarded as high-performing education systems due to the impressive performance of their students in international large-scale assessments. A case in point is the Programme for International Student Assessment (PISA). Shanghai outperformed other countries and economies in 2009 and 2012; Singapore was ranked second for PISA 2009 and 2012 and took the top spot in 2015 (OECD, 2010, 2014). The performance of Shanghai and Singapore is impressive not just in terms of their ranking but also in the wide performance gaps between their scores and the OECD average scores. For example, Shanghai students scored an average of 613 in mathematics in PISA 2012 when the OECD average was 494. Given that 40 points is roughly equivalent to one whole year of schooling, this means that Shanghai students are at least two school years ahead of their peers in mathematics. Singapore students, based on the 2015 PISA data, are at least one school year ahead of their peers in science (556 versus OECD average score of 493), reading (535 versus OECD average score of 493) and mathematics (564 versus the OECD average score of 490) (OECD, 2014).

The consistently remarkable achievements of Shanghai and Singapore have led to these two cities being regarded as reference societies – sites for policy borrowing and learning by other educational jurisdictions (Tan & Reyes, 2017). While there is a growing corpus of works on the educational systems and policies of Shanghai and Singapore, relatively little has been written on the assessment reforms in both jurisdictions. This chapter focuses on recent assessment reforms in Shanghai and Singapore by highlighting their shared aspiration to forward holistic education and formative assessment. This chapter addresses one main question: What are the experiences of two high-performing education systems in attempting to implement assessment reforms?

The first part of the chapter introduces the theoretical framework represented by a marked shift towards viewing assessment that captures more complex aspects of student achievement as opposed to fragmented pieces of knowledge, as well as an emphasis on social and participatory practices of learning in contrast with the widespread use of accumulating seemingly detached achievement results

(James Pellegrino, Noami Chudowsky, & Robert Glaser, 2001a; Shepard, 1992). This is followed by a discussion of major assessment reform initiatives in Shanghai and Singapore. The chapter concludes with the educational implications for policymakers, researchers and educators.

THEORETICAL FRAMEWORK

The Roots of Assessment Reforms

Lorrie Shepard's seminal work on the urgent need to re-visit the longstanding assumptions behind assessment practices serves as one of the theoretical foundations of this chapter. The quote below summarises her main critique of traditional standardised tests:

> Unfortunately much of educational practice, most especially traditional standardised tests, carry forward the assumptions of psychological theories that have since been disproven. Students are still placed in special educational programs, low-ability tracks, readiness rooms, and the like on the bases of static measurements that do not take account of opportunity to learn in calculating ability to profit from instruction. A linear, bit-by-bit skills model of learning is enforced so that students are not allowed to go on thinking until they have mastered the basics. In the name of accountability and educational reform, teachers are forced to spend so much time on the multiple-choice format curriculum that they provide students few of the opportunities that would teach them to think. (Shepard, 1992, p. 327)

Shepard was one of the earliest voices who warned about the potential excesses of large-scale standardised testing, in what she criticised was a practice done "in the name of accountability". Despite the admonitions made by Shepard and her staunch campaign to undertake reforms, the 20th century and particularly its last decade, witnessed the prevalence of what she referred to as assessment principles hinged on outmoded theories. Large-scale testing, employed primarily as a means of choice and distribution of human resources, has become widespread in educational institutions as well as in various sectors of industry. In the specific case of assessment practices used for selection purposes, this was extensively "used in primary and secondary education settings, in selection for university education, in qualification for government civil service positions, and for placement in jobs in the military" (Glaser & Silver, 1994, p. 397). Years later, Shepard's claims of narrowing of the curriculum and the consequent misplaced focus on a limited set of outcomes (Glaser & Silver, 1994), as well as the phenomenon of teachers, teaching to the tests, have been echoed by critical scholars (Au, 2007) as well as by practitioners (Pellegrino et al., 2001).

It comes as no surprise that Shepard's clamor for assessment reforms happened almost at the same time when education systems worldwide were under tremendous pressure from what Michael Apple describes as "an attempt by a new hegemonic bloc to transform our very ideas of the purpose of education" from one that viewed it as a public good to one that was shaped by neoliberal forces driven by competition and the market (Apple, 1993, p. 236). In the United States, then President George Bush called an Education Summit in 1989 to discuss the education crisis in America that was described as a national emergency (Mitchell, 1992). This education reform movement in America established the ethos of accountability in education. One of the tools for ensuring that this was implemented was through the introduction of large-scale testing. In the United Kingdom, under the influence of the New Right and neoliberal perspectives, then Prime Minister Margaret Thatcher promulgated the 1988 Education Reform Act, paving the way for the marketisation of education in Britain or what Stephen Ball describes as "shots in the dark" – policies crafted primarily by dominant ideologies (Ball, 1990, p. 3). A direct consequence of the 1988 British education reform act is the institutionalisation of national testing.

Despite the fact that large-scale testing was firmly enshrined in education systems of the Western world at the close of the 1990s, Shepard's advocacy for assessment reforms did not wane. Her critique sharpened as she warned that assessment practices that were created primarily as accountability measures potentially harmed students and teachers:

High-stakes accountability teaches students that effort in school should be in response to externally administered rewards and punishment rather than the excitement of ideas. And accountability-testing mandates warn teachers to comply or get out (or move, if they can) to schools with higher scoring students (Shepard, 2000a, p. 9).

HOLISTIC EDUCATION AND ASSESSMENT FOR LEARNING

Well into the 21st century and in an education climate driven by a powerful neoliberal ethos, typified by "the celebration of the virtues of the private and market-driven schools" (Tan & Reyes, 2016, p. 23), the influence of assessments has intensified not only as a tool for accountability but worse, as a lever for competition. Within this context, this chapter argues that Shanghai and Singapore – currently positioned as two of the leading education jurisdictions in the world – seem to have paid attention to the need to undertake assessment reforms and have taken concrete steps towards accomplishing these.

On the one hand, Shanghai has affirmed that its current education situation is not ideal and that it is in need of changes. One can contend that Shanghai possesses an "exam-driven, time-consuming, and stressful education system" which has invariably "generated widespread public dissatisfaction with the local education model for the past few decades" (Tan & Reyes, 2018, p. 67). On the other hand, Singapore has recognised the need to search for reforms as it faces a complex and uncertain future. It can be argued that Singapore has "embraced the goal of achieving new economic competencies dealing with creativity and innovation while clinging to high-stakes testing as the prime yardstick of meritocracy" (Reyes & Gopinathan, 2015, p. 152).

This chapter contends that the assessment reforms currently being implemented by Shanghai and Singapore are informed by two core principles: firstly, a marked shift towards viewing assessment that captures more complex aspects of student achievement as opposed to fragmented pieces of knowledge (Pellegrino, Chudowsky, & Glaser, 2001) or in other words, a more holistic view of education. And a second emphasis is on social and participatory practices of learning, in contrast with the widespread use of accumulating seemingly detached achievement results or in other words, a turn towards assessment for learning (Shepard, 2000a).

Our chapter categorically states that Shanghai and Singapore are moving towards embracing assessments that feature some aspects of holistic educative characteristics. Pellegrino, Chudowsky, and Glaser (2001) suggest that assessment needs to be firmly established upon contemporary theories of learning that address how knowledge operates within the cognitive functions of the human mind. The adherence to cognitive processes of learning, they argue, also needs to be closely-linked to the design of assessments, as noted by Pellegrino, Chudowsky, and Glaser (2001):

> Any assessment is based on three interconnected elements or foundations: the aspects of achievement that are to be assessed (cognition), the tasks used to collect evidence about students' achievement (observation), and the methods used to analyse the evidence resulting from the tasks (interpretation). To understand and improve educational assessment, the principles and beliefs underlying each of these elements as well as their interrelationships, must be made explicit. (p. 20)

The explicit interplay of cognition, observation and interpretation results in fresh perspectives of viewing assessments. It requires a "move beyond a focus on component skills and discrete bits of knowledge to encompass the more complex aspects of student achievement" which is how traditional assessments have been carried out, as well as an increasing recognition of the need to adopt "social dimensions of learning, including social and participatory practices that support knowing and understanding" (Pellegrino et al., 2001, p. 102). In other words, assessments should be seen as an exercise that necessitates a more complex and holistic approach.

Our chapter also makes a fundamental claim that that Shanghai and Singapore are shifting some of the components of their respective testing regimes towards specific aspects of assessment for learning. The basis for this emanates from two contemporary developments in cognitive psychology, namely, the realisation that: (1) intelligence is and can be developed; and (2) that all learning requires thinking (Shepard, 1992, p. 326) through social-constructivist approaches. Shepard proposes two fundamental changes in the way tests are undertaken in order for it to genuinely be directed towards assessment for learning:

First, its form and content must be changed to better represent important thinking and problem-solving skills in each of the disciplines. This means assessing learning based on observations, oral questioning, significant tasks, projects, demonstrations, collections of student work, and students' self-evaluations, and it means that teachers must engage in systematic analysis of the available evidence. Second, the way that assessment is used in classrooms and how it is regarded by teachers and students must change. This literally calls for a change in the culture of classrooms so that students no longer try to feign competence or work to perform well on the test as an end separate from real learning. Instead, students and teachers should collaborate in assessing prior knowledge, probing apparent misconceptions, and resolving areas of confusion because it is agreed that such assessments will help students understand better. Students should engage in self-assessment not only to take responsibility for their own learning but to develop metacognitive skills by learning to apply the standards that define quality work in a field to their own work (Shepard, 2000b, p. 66).

In the succeeding sections, examples of assessment reforms in Shanghai and Singapore are presented. These reforms centre around the push towards introducing certain aspects of holistic education as well as specific initiatives to spark changes towards assessment for learning.

ASSESSMENT REFORMS IN SHANGHAI AND SINGAPORE

The assessment reforms in both Shanghai and Singapore are geared towards reducing exam stress and promoting new forms of assessment. Although Shanghai and Singapore have excelled in international large-scale assessments, a perennial challenge in both societies is an exam-oriented culture that underscores test scores and academic performance (Tan, 2017a, 2017b). The overriding importance of the education system in Shanghai and Singapore as well as in other similar regions in East Asia is "predominantly dictated by the examination system" (Li, 2010, p. 41). One can trace the historical roots of this very strong belief to the "Chinese civil service examination system established in the seventh century to select the most able and moral individuals to serve the royal court" (Li, 2010, p. 41).

Terminal, high-stakes exams characterise the schooling system in Shanghai and Singapore. Shanghai students need to sit for two public exams: zhongkao (senior secondary school entrance exam) at the end of junior secondary level, and gaokao (national college entrance exam) at the end of senior secondary level. Singapore students need to sit for three public exams: PSLE (primary school leaving exam) at the end of primary level, GCE 'O' Level at the end of secondary level (although small group of students who are enrolled in the six-year integrated programme are exempted from this exam), and GCE 'A' Level or other qualifications at the end of the high school level.

The high-stakes nature of the above-mentioned exams has generated much stress in the students, parents and teachers in both Shanghai and Singapore. At the same time, the significant time and effort demanded of students to prepare for these exams means that other aspects of education such as physical health, mental and emotional wellbeing and artistic talents are neglected. In their desire to advance holistic education, the education authorities in both Shanghai and Singapore have embarked on a series of assessment reforms in their respective localities. Due to space constraint, this chapter shall focus on the major assessment reforms in recent years. In both Shanghai and Singapore, the reform goals are to champion holistic education and formative assessment.

Shanghai

The assessment reforms in Shanghai are directed at actualising two objectives: changes to the gaokao; and introduction of alternative assessment modes in schools. The gaokao reform aims to reduce the stress of high-stakes exams, champion broad-based learning and direct higher educational institutions to take a more comprehensive approach towards student admissions (Shanghai Municipal Education Commission, 2014; Centre on International Education Benchmarking, 2015; Gu & Magaziner, 2016). There are three main changes to the gaokao system. First, the gaokao system has been changed from '3+X' to '3+3' model: students will still sit for the usual three compulsory subjects of Chinese, mathematics and English, but they now have to take three instead of one elective.

And unlike the previous system where the choice of elective was restricted to a disciplinary specialisation (sciences or humanities), students from 2017 will no longer specialise in either the sciences or the humanities. Instead, they can choose to be tested on any three subjects from the sciences such as chemistry and physics, as well as from the humanities such as geography and history (Yan, 2014). Secondly, the electives will not be tested alongside the compulsory subjects during the gaokao exam in June. Instead, students will sit for the electives exams prior to high school graduation at the Ordinary Senior Secondary Level Academic Standard Graded Exam (putong gaozhong xueye shuiping dengjixing kaoshi) (also known as Academic Proficiency Test or APT). Thirdly, students can take the English language paper twice (once in January and once in June) and use the higher score for consideration in admission. The English language paper will also add listening and speaking components to the written format.

The second major assessment reform measure focuses on the enactment of formative assessment in Shanghai schools. Two prominent initiatives are school-based curriculum and Green Academic Evaluation System. Schools are given the autonomy to design and launch an array of courses, programmes and activities that cater for the diverse needs and interests of their students. Alongside the new courses, programmes and activities under the school-based curriculum are alternative and formative assessment modes. Students are evaluated on their performance of real-life tasks through experiments, oral presentations, poster displays and research projects (Shen, 2007; Tan, 2013). Of special mention among the new alternative assessment method is the 'integrated quality appraisal' (zonghe suzhi pingjia) that is geared towards holistic education.

This appraisal evaluates individual students based on the following aspects: the development of ideological and moral character, cultivation of traditional Chinese culture, courses taken and academic results obtained, innovative spirit and practical ability, physical and mental health, interests and talents (Shanghai Municipal Education

Commission, 2014). To ensure reliability and validity, schools are reminded to "objectively record the student's growth process" and "comprehensively reflect" on the student's all-rounded development (Shanghai Municipal Education Commission, 2014).

Unlike summative exams, the integrated quality appraisal is formative as it accumulates the daily and all-rounded growth and achievement of students throughout their learning years. Using both quantitative and qualitative measurements, this appraisal enables students understand their own strengths and areas of improvement under the guidance of teachers (Tan, 2013). Teachers should track the students' learning process and developmental progress through the 'Growth Record Booklet' by taking note of the latter's moral quality, citizenship quality, learning ability, social interaction and cooperation, and participation in sports, health and aesthetics (Shanghai Municipal Education Commission, 2006).

Another initiative to promote alternative assessment is the Green Academic Evaluation System (lüse xueye zhibiao pingjia tixi). This system aspires to change the prevailing exam-oriented mind-set in Shanghai by focusing on not just the students' academic results but also their physical and mental health as well as moral conduct. The Green Indices were first carried out in 2011 for a total sample size of 63, 640 students from Grade 4 and Grade 9, as well as 9445 teachers and 804 principals across Shanghai (Wang, 2012). A total of ten indicators are used in the Green Academic Evaluation System, with academic performance comprising only one out of ten criteria (Shanghai Municipal Education Commission, 2011). The ten indicators are different indexes that measure students' academic standard, students' learning motivation, students' schoolwork burden, teacher-student relationship, teachers' teaching methods, principal's curriculum leadership, impact of students' socio-economic background on their academic performance, moral character, students' physical and mental health, and improvement.

Singapore

In Singapore, the assessment reforms are similarly targeted at promoting holistic education and formative assessment. But instead of reforming the gaokao, as in the case of Shanghai, the Ministry of Education (MOE) in Singapore turns its attention to the PSLE. It was announced in 2006 that a new PSLE scoring system will be introduced with effect from 2021 (MOE, 2016). The rationale of the revised PSLE scoring system is to develop well-rounded individuals by encouraging "more students to discover their strengths and interests, as well as strengthen their values, knowledge and skills needed to succeed in the future" (MOE, n.d.). Instead of assessing each student's exam performance using precise marks, broad bands known as an 'achievement level' (AL) will be utilised.

This means that a student who scores 90 and above for each subject will be awarded with an AL of 1, a student who scores 85–89 will be awarded an AL of 2, and so on. There will be a total of 8 ALs from 1 (marks of 90 and above) to 8 (below 20 marks). A student's total score will be the sum of the ALs of each subject, with 4 being the best possible result. Instead of grading students in relation to how their peers perform which is employed in the existing PSLE system, the new system will award the ALs to students regardless of how their counterparts perform. This change serves to help children and their parents to "focus on their own learning instead of trying to outdo others" (MOE, 2006).

Besides changes to the PSLE scoring system, the education authority has also implemented measures to encourage holistic and formative assessments. Secondary students are given more choices to decide on their subject combination in schools, and could even study new subjects such as Economics, Computer Studies and Drama. The post-secondary curriculum is also revised to develop thinking skills and nurturing the spirit and values required for Singaporeans to thrive in a more globalised, innovation driven future (MOE, 2005).

The goal is to provide a broad-based education where students are exposed to and be able to excel in different disciplines and ways of learning. There is also a deliberate shift from emphasising summative assessment to formative assessment. The MOE values students' holistic development of competencies such as critical thinking, innovation and creativity, communication, collaboration, independent learning, lifelong learning, information and communication technology, and active citizenship (MOE, 2016). As such, alternative forms of assessment, such as project work and Science Practical Assessment have been introduced as school-based assessments into Singaporean classrooms at various key stages of schooling. At the secondary school level, coursework is also recommended as a school-based assessment. Coursework marks count toward the final grades in the examination of subject areas including Design and Technology, Food and Nutrition, Art, and Music (Tan, Koh, & Choy, 2017).

Another major initiative known as C2015 has been launched by MOE to centre on the development of students' dispositions: a confident individual, a self-directed learner, an active citizen, and a concerned contributor (MOE, 2016). In the Primary Education Review and Implementation (PERI) recommendation (MOE, 2009), the exams at primary 1 and 2 have been replaced with 'bite-sized assessment' or 'topical tests', with an eye towards using assessment to support student learning. Likewise, the Secondary Education Review and Implementation (SERI) recommendation emphasises the inculcation of learning and life skills, values, character and citizenship, and socio-emotional competencies among secondary school students (MOE, 2010). Many of these soft skills involve processes and cannot be assessed by one-shot, traditional standardised paper-and-pen tests; instead, formative, authentic and school-based assessments have become viable alternatives (Koh & Luke, 2009).

DISCUSSION AND IMPLICATIONS

The attempts at reforming high-stakes tests represented by the gaokao in Shanghai and the PSLE in Singapore are laudable but we argue that these are at best preliminary steps towards achieving authentic holistic forms of assessment. In the Shanghai case, the change from a more restrictive and limited test regime to a slightly more open and flexible approach satisfies Pellegrino et al.'s first two suggestions of cognition (broader range of subjects to be assessed) and observation (a diversity of sources to determine student achievement). However, in the third component of interpretation (variety of methods used to analyse and report results), the Shanghai reforms seem to have remained in the traditional realm, where the gaokao remains as a tool to be employed as a university placement system.

In the Singapore case, the projected reforms for the PSLE in 2021 are promising and manages to satisfy Pellegrino et al.'s second and third components. Observation is achieved with the move to diversify the sources used to determine student achievement, particularly with the focus on knowledge, skills and values. Interpretation is also accomplished through the variety of methods used to analyse and report results, particularly the encouraging change in shifting towards criterion-based referencing. However, the first component of Cognition – in the Singapore context persists, where PSLE, we argue still remains as a potent tool in placement system for young learners in secondary school contexts. The current manifestations of holistic assessment reforms in the Shanghai and Singapore contexts also do not address another key feature identified by Pellegrino et al.: the need to recognise social and participatory dimensions of learning that can be incorporated in authentic holistic assessments.

It must be made clear that the implementation of assessment reforms that involve holistic approaches does not come easy. In the first place, assessments that are designed in a truly comprehensive manner require that these be undertaken in authentic situations (Mabry, 1999). Considering that schools are increasingly becoming an "artificial environment" of learning, particularly in 21st century contexts (Reyes, 2015, p. 378), achieving a match between truly holistic assessments and authentic situations remains elusive. Another limitation to the full implementation of holistic assessments involves the role that teachers play. Given that promoting truly all-rounded evaluations of student work requires a great amount of subjectivity among teachers, there is a tendency to revert to "preferred formula-based methods" (Shepard, 2000a, p. 6) in order to avoid the pressure of being seen as biased.

The assessment reforms of Shanghai and Singapore designed to foster assessment for learning – represented by the Green Academic Evaluation System in Shanghai and the collective set of initiatives that include Project Work and Science Practical Assessments and the introduction of Soft Skills in Singapore – are commendable. Furthermore, we argue that these are examples of worthy works-in progress.

In the case of Shanghai, the introduction of a wide variety of assessment tasks and modes (i.e. performances, real-life tasks, poster displays) satisfies Shepard's first of two recommendations to better represent important thinking and problem-solving skills in the move towards assessment for learning. Also, Shanghai's attempts to incorporate both quantitative and qualitative measurements of students' progress are a positive step towards the second and final recommendation of Shepard that speaks of the need to change the culture of classrooms. In the Singapore context, the assessment reforms that place students' initiatives (i.e. student-initiated project work and science practical assessments) at the forefront clearly satisfy Shepard's first point of addressing thinking and problem solving skills.

However, the domineering presence of the PSLE as well as the "N", "O" and "A" Level tests for secondary school learners effectively hamper moves towards genuinely changing classroom cultures. It should be pointed out that building upon Pellegrino et al.'s suggestions of incorporating the students' voices themselves, policy initiatives that recognise social and participatory dimensions of learning in Shanghai and Singapore could move Shanghai and Singapore's assessment reform initiatives closer to Shepard's second ideal of achieving genuine changes in classroom cultures.

In regard to pursuing authentic assessment for learning, there remain very real obstacles that confront Shanghai and Singapore – as well as other education systems – in their intention to implementing these changes. The first obstacle concerns teachers. Shepard captures the sentiment succinctly, arguing that in efforts to embrace assessment for learning "it is important to recognise the pervasive negative effects of accountability tests and the extent to which externally imposed testing programs prevent and drive out thoughtful classroom practices" (Shepard, 2000a, p. 9).

The next obstacle focuses on the most important stakeholder in education – the learners themselves. Given the fact that assessment for learning is designed to ensure that students "keep learning and remain confident that they can continue to learn at productive levels if they keep trying to learn" existing school mechanisms and infrastructure must support these young learners instead of propagating current negative practices that constantly push students towards unnecessary "frustration or hopelessness" (Stiggins, 2002, p. 760).

CONCLUSION

This chapter presented an account of how two successful education jurisdictions, namely Shanghai and Singapore, contend with issues and challenges pertaining to their existing assessment and testing systems. The initial section of the chapter provided a brief description of the current state of assessment regimes in both contexts: on the one hand, Shanghai is seen as primarily an exam-driven, time-consuming and stressful education context. On the other, Singapore is viewed as a nation in contradiction, locked in an entrenched ethos of meritocracy tied to high-stakes testing whilst attempting to embrace 21st century competencies. An explanation of the theoretical roots of the assessment reforms being introduced in both contexts then followed. Two components were explained in detail. First, the notion of holistic types of testing and secondly, assessment for learning – both of which were founded on contemporary theories of social-cognitive learning. The succeeding section outlined specific examples of how Shanghai and Singapore attempted to implement assessment reforms. The penultimate section provided a discussion of issues and challenges faced by both these contexts as they continue to implement these assessment reforms.

This chapter provided a cursory glance at the state of testing regimes in Shanghai and Singapore using the theoretical lens of reforms that hinged on holistic approaches and assessment for learning. Issues in relation to selected assessment reforms in both contexts were identified. Challenges faced by both Singapore and Shanghai in implementing these reforms were similarly outlined. For purposes of further careful study, this chapter proposes two possible areas of inquiry:

1. Studies that measure the validity and reliability of these novel forms of assessments. On paper, the theory of holistic assessment coupled with assessment for learning underpinned by social learning theories sounds convincing. But it would be relevant and most insightful if fellow researchers and practitioners explore the validity and reliability of these novel types of assessments.
2. We also propose the conduct of in-depth explorations of how the most important stakeholders – students – see themselves within the dynamics of these new forms of assessment. In the current initiatives of Singapore and Shanghai, students' voices are silent. This is not a surprise since most studies on assessment reforms usually focus on systems and teachers, in the process silencing young learners. For an issue that concerns them most, we believe that hearing their voices is paramount. In conclusion, most of the educational transformations being carried out by Shanghai and Singapore are in their incipient stages. As both nations lead the way as exemplars of highly-successful education systems, the eyes of observers and education stakeholders in general are on them as they boldly move forward in their continuing attempts to undertake assessment reforms.

REFERENCES

Apple, M. (1993). The politics of official knowledge: Does a national curriculum make sense? *Teachers College Record, 95*(2), 222–241.

Ball, S. (1990). *Politics and policymaking in education.* London: Routledge.

Centre on International Education Benchmarking. (2015). *Shanghai-China.* Retrieved November 11, 2016, from http://www.ncee.org/programs-affiliates/center-on-international-education-benchmarking/ top-performing-countries/shanghai-china/shanghai-china-instructional-systems/

Glaser, R., & Silver, E. (1994). Assessment, testing and instruction: Retrospect and prospect. *Review of Research in Education, 20,* 393–419.

Gu, M., & Magaziner, J. (2016, May 2). The gaokao: History, reform, and rising international significance of China's National College entrance examination. *World Education News & Reviews.* Retrieved November 11, 2016, from http://wenr.wes.org/2016/05/the-gaokao-history-reform-and-international-significance-of-chinas-national-college-entrance-examination

Koh, K., & Luke, A. (2009). Authentic and conventional assessment in Singapore schools: An empirical study of teacher assignments and student work. *Assessment in Education: Principles, Policy & Practice, 16*(3), 291–318.

Li, J. (2010). Learning to self-perfect: Chinese beliefs about learning. In C. Chan & N. Rao (Eds.), *Revisiting the Chinese learner: Changing contexts, changing education* (pp. 35–70). Hong Kong: Springer and the Comparative Education Research Centre of the University of Hong Kong.

Mabry, L. (1999). Writing to the rubric: Lingering effects of traditional standardised testing on direct writing assessment. *Phi Delta Kappan, 80*(9), 673–679.

Ministry of Education. (2005). *Breath and flexibility: The new 'A' level curriculum 2006.* Retrieved May 15, 2006, from http://www.moe.gov.sg/cpdd/alevel2006/

Ministry of Education. (2009). *Report of the primary education review and implementation committee.* Singapore: Ministry of Education.

Ministry of Education. (2010). *Report of the secondary review and implementation committee.* Singapore: Ministry of Education.

Mitchell, R. (1992). *Testing for learning: How new approaches to evaluation can improve American schools.* New York, NY: The Free Press.

MOE. (2016). *Changes to the PSLE scoring and secondary one posting from 2021.* Retrieved November 8, 2017, from https://www.moe.gov.sg/microsites/psle/PSLE%20Scoring/psle-scoring.html

Pellegrino, J., Chudowsky, N., & Glaser, R. (2001a). *Knowing what students know: The science and design of educational assessment.* Washington, DC: National Academies Press.

Reyes, V. (2015). How do school leaders navigate ICT educational reform? Policy learning narratives from a Singapore context. *International Journal of Leadership in Education, 18*(3), 365–385.

Reyes, V., & Gopinathan, S. (2015). A critique of knowledge-based economies: A case study of Singapore education stakeholders. *International Journal of Educational Reform, 24*(2), 136–159.

Shanghai Live. (2015, June 16). *Heavy rain on second day of gaokao* [video clip]. Retrieved October 12, 2016, from https://www.youtube.com/watch?v=1ZiA4qY8THQ

Shanghai Municipal Education Commission. (2006). *Shanghaishi zhongxiao xueshen zhonghe sushi pingjia fangan (shixing) de tongzhi* [Notice on Shanghai city's secondary and primary school student's comprehensive appraisal plan]. Retrieved February 4, 2011, from http://www.ptq.sh.gov.cn/gb/shpt/node4343/node4349/node4649/node4668/node4672/userobject1ai56455.html

Shanghai Municipal Education Commission. (2011). *Shanghaishi jiaoyu weiyuanhui guanyu 'Shangahishi zhongxiao xuesheng xueye zhiliang lǜse zhibiao (shixing)' de shishi yijian* [Opinions of the Shanghai Education Commission on the implementation of 'Green Indicators for the academic quality of primary and secondary school students in Shanghai' (trial)]. Retrieved June 2, 2016, from http://www.shmec.gov.cn/html/xxgk/201111/402152011007.php

Shanghai Municipal Education Commission. (2014). *Shanghai shi shenhua gaodeng xuexiao kaoshi zhaosheng zonghe gaige shishi fangan* [Implementation plan to deepen the comprehensive reform for college entrance exam in Shanghai city]. Retrieved November 11, 2016, from http://gaokao.eol.cn/zui_xin_dong_tai_2939/20140919/t20140919_1177783.shtml

Shen, X. (2007). *Shanghai education.* Singapore: Thomson Learning.

Shepard, L. (1992). Commentary: What policy makers who mandate tests should know about the new pyschology of intellectual ability and learning. In B. R. Gifford & M. C. O'Conner (Eds.), *Changing assessments: Alternative views of aptitude, achievement, and instruction* (pp. 302–327). Boston, MA: Kluwer Academic Publishers.

Shepard, L. (2000a). The role of assessment in a learning culture. *Educational Research, 29*(7), 4–14.

Shepard, L. (2000b). *The role of classroom assessment in teaching and learning.* Boulder, CO: CRESTT/Universtiy of Colorado at Boulder.

Stiggins, R. (2002). Assessment crisis: The absence of assessment for learning. *Phi Delta Kappan, 83*(10), 758–765.

Tan, C. (2013). *Learning from Shanghai: Lessons on achieving educational success* (p. 245). Dordrecht: Springer.

Tan, C. (2017a). Chinese responses to Shanghai's performance in PISA. *Comparative Education, 53*(2), 209–223.

Tan, C. (2017b). The enactment of the policy initiative for critical thinking in Singapore schools. *Journal of Education Policy, 32*(5), 588–603.

Tan, C., Koh, K., & Choy, W. (2016). The education system in Singapore. In S. Juszczyk (Ed.), *Asian education systems* (pp. 129–148). Toruñ: Adam Marszalek Publishing House.

Tan, C., & Reyes, V. (2016). Neo-liberal education policy in China. In S. Guo & Y. Guo (Eds.), *Spotlight on China: Changes in education under China's market economy* (pp. 19–33). Rotterdam, The Netherlands: Sense Publishers.

Tan, C., & Reyes, V. (2018). Shanghai-China and the emergence of a global reference society. In L. Volante (Ed.), *The PISA effect on global educational governance* (pp. 61–75). New York, NY: Routledge.

Wang Y. (2012, October). Shanghai shi zongxiao xuesheng xueye zhiliang lüse zhibiao tixi de shishi ji fansi [The implementation and reflection of the green index system for the academic quality of secondary and primary students in Shanghai]. *Xuexiao Guanli Yu Fazhan.*

Yan. (2014, September 20). Shanghai, Zhejiang to pilot gaokao reforms. *China Daily.* Retrieved November 11, 2016, from http://usa.chinadaily.com.cn/china/2014-09/20/content_18632195.htm

Vicente Reyes
University of Queensland
Australia

Charlene Tan
Nanyang Technological University
Singapore

MARK RUSSELL, HELEN BAREFOOT, BRYAN TAYLOR
AND LEIGH POWELL

4. THE ESCAPE PROJECT

Background, Sustainability and Transferability

INTRODUCTION

Student satisfaction data derived from instruments such as the UK National Student Survey (NSS) have created a wake-up call to many universities. This wake-up call is amplified when we note that that the NSS data are being used in public-facing university league tables, and components of the NSS data are also included in information made available to prospective students i.e. the Unistats Data Set. (HEFCE, 2017). Additionally, the UK Government's 2016 White Paper 'Higher education: success as a knowledge economy' paved the way for the Teaching Excellence Framework (TEF). At Phase 1, the TEF submissions from participating universities resulted in an institution-wide indicator of teaching excellence. The indicator being denoted as Gold, Silver or Bronze.

For some universities, notably some of the Gold and Silver rated university, the rating is displayed in university web sites and email signatures. Importantly and beyond the marketing potential of a Gold or Silver rating, the result of the institutional TEF award (aspects of which comprise NSS data) is linked to the level at which universities can set tuition fees. As such, both primarily (via NSS league tables and KIS) and secondarily (via the TEF and hence fee income), the NSS has focused the need for institutional responses to areas of less than satisfactory student experiences. Simply put, the NSS is important to universities from both reputational and financial perspectives.

In relation to this chapter, explorations of the NSS will highlight Assessment and Feedback as being the least favored aspect of the students' educational experience. In addition to Assessment and Feedback, the themes of the NSS are Teaching, Learning Opportunities, Organization and Management, Learning Resources, Learning Community and Student Voice. Whilst there are numerous critiques of the NSS and, in relation to assessment, the less-than-ideal satisfaction data is arguably likely to be expected, i.e. there cannot be too many students with a strong desire to be sat in examination hall for two or three hours and have their work judged, the NSS data on Assessment and Feedback is troubling.

Beyond the troubling impact on league tables and TEF results, it is especially troubling given the importance of assessment on matters such as student motivation, student study patterns and student approaches to learning have long been recognized Snyder (1970), Millar and Partlet (1974) and Biggs and Tang (2011). Indeed, when presenting their simple-yet-elegant model of constructive alignment (i.e. the three components of (i) intended learning outcome, (ii) designed teaching activities and (iii) designed assessment activities), Biggs and Tang (ibid.) identify the criticality of assessment when he asserts "assessment is the senior partner [in constructive alignment], get it wrong and the rest collapses".

Helpfully, many faculty are acutely aware of both student dissatisfaction with assessment and its dominant influence on study behaviors and learning. As such many faculty have designed and implemented new and innovative assessment activity to respond to some of the ongoing challenges. Such challenges include how to create assessment activity that is both educationally effective and resource efficient; how to ensure assessment responds to the personal needs of the learner as class sizes increase and; how to ensure that feedback is meaningful, timely and can be demonstrably used to support learning in upcoming assessment tasks.

A number of these course-related assessment innovations have been evaluated and disseminated through peer reviewed outlets such as conferences and journals. An additional challenge in creating meaningful student assessment is not necessarily with the personal commitment of faculty to review and change assessment within a course, but rather the ways in which courses cohere and create a programmatic assessment strategy. For instance, it is the program (not the course) that defines the student's actual assessment experience and journey; it is at the program level (not course level) that we see if courses are disparate and discrete entities or are truly part of an interconnected whole; and it is at the program level (not course level) that we better understand the collective assessment intentions. Hence, as helpful as it is that individual faculty are reflecting on their assessment activity and creating new assessment innovations, there remains a need to develop and ensure coherent programmatic perspective exists.

Whilst programs of study in the UK will be designed in ways that take account of the UK Quality Code (and the associated Subject Benchmark Statements) (QAA, 2018) program designers may create program documents that do not fully articulate assessment as a programmatic strategy. i.e. some program documents may simply describe the ways in which course assessment is to be handled and how the assessment aligns with the intended learning outcomes of the program and those of its constituent courses. Such descriptions will never truly offer a program assessment vision or strategy but will focus more on how assessment is operationalized within the courses. Even for those programs that have been more deliberate in designing and articulating a programmatic assessment vision and strategy, there exists much potential to drift from the original programmatic intent. Such potential arises because formal program reviews typically operate on a five year cycle. During this time period faculty teaching arrangements and duties may change, new faculty may be deployed and minor curriculum and assessment modifications are possible that do not always require oversight of the program leadership team. Hence, it remains possible that the assessment intentions are 'owned' at the course level which increases the potential for 'course myopia'.

In terms of curriculum developments, a few UK universities have deployed a number of change management approaches. Such approaches have the intent for the curriculum design process to be collaborative and participatory; the benefits being building a shared consensus and collective ownership of the design. See for example the Change Academy of Blended Learning Enhancement (Anderson et al., 2008), Carpe Diem (Salmon, 2015) and DDI (Seeto & Vlachopoulos, 2015). Such social approaches to curriculum design and curriculum redesign could also be developed and applied to the assessment domain too. The notion of being social, in this context refers to the fact that assessment is not just designed, seen and reviewed by the small program leadership team but rather by the entire program teaching team.

Having set out a context and identified a potential need for assessment to be developed more programmatically, socially and collaboratively, the remaining sections of this chapter outline an approach to assessment design that is deliberately programmatic and social and then identifies how the original approach has been sustained (and enhanced in the initial university) and diffused for wider benefit in other universities.

THE ESCAPE PROJECT

The Effecting Sustainable Change in Assessment Practice and Experience (ESCAPE) Project was conceived, designed and led by a team at the University of Hertfordshire (UK). The project was part of the two year Transforming Curriculum Design and Delivery Through Technology Program funded by the UK Joint Information System Committee (Jisc). The Jisc program explicitly set out to create changes in curriculum design and delivery and create systematic change at an institutional level. As implied by its name, the ESCAPE Project set out with similar intentions whilst also creating approaches and tools that could be considered and potentially used by other institutions.

Accepting that the ESCAPE project team have already published aspects of the work, see for example Russell and Bygate (2010) and Russell, Barefoot, and Bygate (2013), for completeness some of key features of the ESCAPE Project are listed below and include

- Using research informed principles/themes
- Using Appreciative Inquiry when working with program teams
- Being programmatic and seeking to break any notions of course myopia
- Creating a social framework for assessment design/redesign
- Looking for good assessment practice (and linking current practice to principles)
- Partnership working between the core (project) team, the program (curriculum) teams and students.

The research informed themes, referred to as the ESCAPE (Assessment for Learning) Themes, drew on the work of Nicol and MacFarlane-Dick (2006), Gibbs and Simpson (2004), and were inspired by the simplicity and utility of Chickering and

Gamson's Seven Principles of Good Practice in Undergraduate Education (1987). As such, the ESCAPE project argued, and used a frame of reference the idea that:

Good Assessment for Learning
- Engages students with the assessment criteria
- Supports personalised learning
- Stimulates dialogue
- Ensures feedback leads to improvement
- Focuses on student development
- Considers student and faculty effort

Appreciative Inquiry (AI) was used as an evaluation methodology to help the ESCAPE project team gain an understanding of the current status and build constructive relationships with the program team (faculty). Appreciate Inquiry typically uses four linked phases, these being the Discover, Dream, Design and Deliver phases. Additionally, one of the core principles of AI is the importance of being positive and focusing on the current strengths and not the deficits of the situation being evaluated. Within the AI framework, examples of the ESCAPE activity includes:

- Conducting one to one interviews with faculty in which faculty were asked to describe the strengths of their assessment practice and how we might sustain and/ or grow the strengths in other areas of the program.
- Using various visual representations of assessment activity to provoke programmatic and pedagogical discussions without being value laden nor focusing on any deficit.
- Capturing the current descriptions of assessment and overlaying the ESCAPE themes on the current practice.
- Collaboratively and socially identifying a new assessment future.

VISUALIZATION AND SOCIALIZATION TOOLS OF THE ESCAPE PROJECT

Two primary visualization approaches were developed to help create a programmatic perspective of assessment. These approaches were:

- Assessment Timeline and Assessment Landscapes
- Assessment Loading Map

The Assessment Timelines identifies when the assessment occurs in the term, the relative weighting of the assessment (to overall grade), and the 'in-course' assessment connections (see for example Figure 4.1).

The Assessment Landscape, identifies how the assessments connect to other assessments outside of the course (see Figures 4.2 and 4.3).

For reference, the circles represents the assessment activity and its color represents its weighting to the course. Green circles represent a low stakes assessment task <15%, orange circles represents a medium stakes assessment task 16–40%, whereas a red circle represents a high stakes assessment task > 41%.

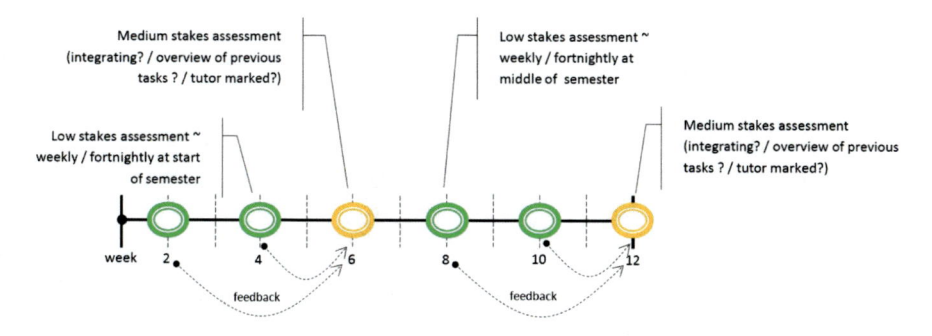

Figure 4.1. An example Assessment Timeline (assessment within a course)

Fictitious-yet-authentic Assessment Timelines have been produced to show some alternative assessment patterns and notably the likely consequences. These fictitious Assessment Timelines have been clustered in the three themes.

- Moving away from high stakes end of process assessment
- Making more of feedback
- Developing a Programmatic perspective (the Assessment Landscape)

The Assessment Landscapes were helpful in seeing any assessment bunching, and also if and where feedback from assessment within one course impacted on the assessment in another course (see Figures 4.2 and 4.3 for examples).

Note in Figure 4.3 that the links between assessment have been identified as they occur at different levels of study. These links could relate to items of developing complexity in the subject or in the transferable skills being developed from one course to another.

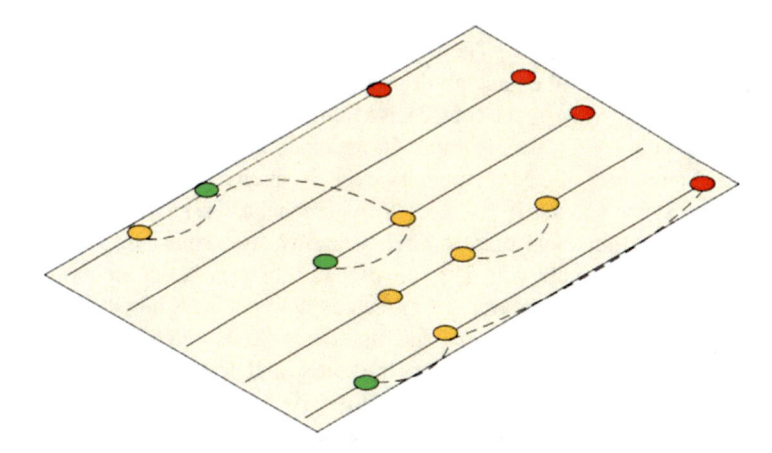

Figure 4.2. An example partial Assessment Landscape
(assessment across courses at one level of study)

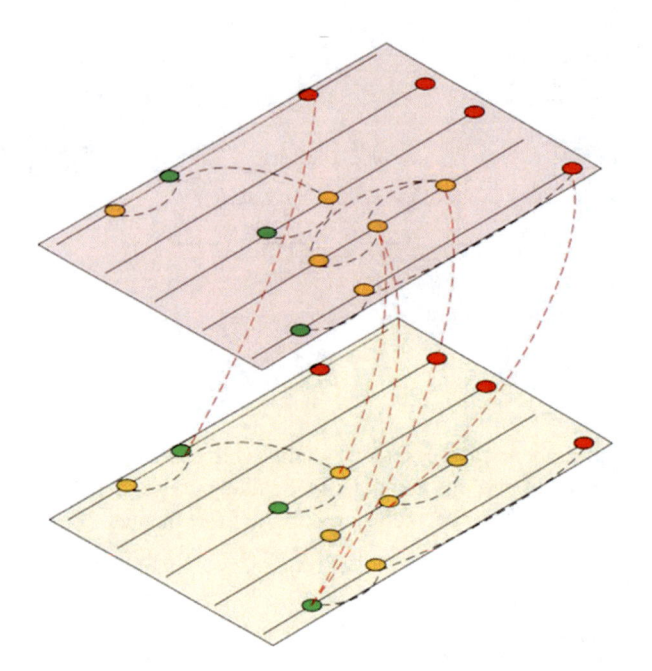

*Figure 4.3. An example Assessment Landscape
(assessment across courses at two levels of study)*

The Assessment Map was used to represent the number of assessment tasks within a course and importantly the overall weighting of the examination for each course within a program. An example of which is shown in Figure 4.4.

In Figure 4.4, each pie chart represents the total assessment within a course. Segments of the pie charts are color coded to represent the different assessment types that exists in the course. The horizontal axis represents the weighting of the examination to the overall course grade. Hence, pie charts located towards the right hand side of the Map indicate the course has a high examination weighing. The vertical axis represents the level (year) of study. In the example presented in Figure 4.4 you can see the dominance of examination at Level 6 (which differs from levels 5 and 4) and the fact that each course in level 6 has an identical assessment diet.

These visualization tools present already known assessment data in a visually appealing and programmatic way. They are used to help team-based explorations of the assessment activity so that program teams can explore the ways in which each course uses assessment to leverage learning and also the ways in which the program offers assessment interactions within and across the course and hence assessment coherence.

The ESCAPE project team worked initially with programs in the School of Life Sciences and The Business School and also set about running a university wide project seeking to reduce the reliance on end of process high stakes examinations (across all Schools of study).

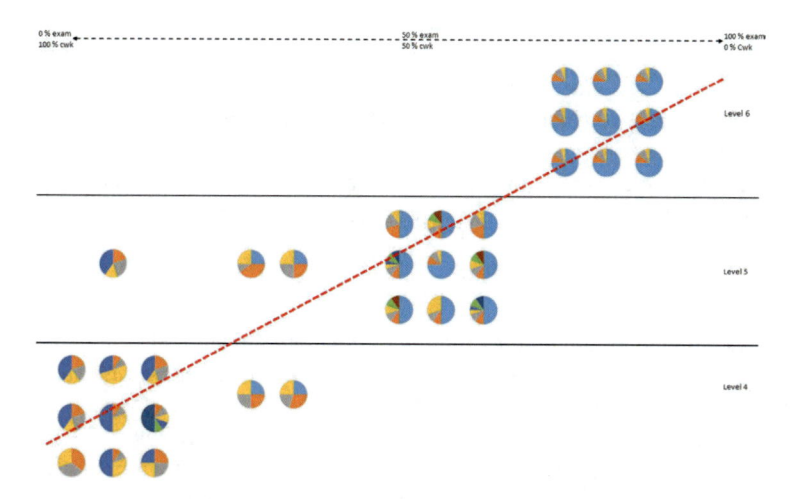

Figure 4.4. An example of an Assessment Map

SUSTAINABILITY AT THE UNIVERSITY OF HERTFORDSHIRE

The ESCAPE project team were keen to embed and sustain the change and benefits rather than just create local and temporary improvement. Given this intent, at the end of the ESCAPE project funding, the University of Hertfordshire used a number of approaches to ensure the ESCAPE project continued to have a positive and institution-wide impact. These approaches included:

Embedding ESCAPE Ideals in Institutional Quality Assurance/Quality Enhancement Processes

All program teams are now required to include a Program Assessment Strategy within their validation/periodic review submission document which details how the ESCAPE Assessment for Learning themes are met within the program. Additionally, program teams must develop and include an Assessment Landscape within their validation/periodic review submission and following approval, the Assessment Landscape must be annually updated once the program is running,

To exemplify the Assessment for Learning themes, the Learning and Teaching Innovation Center developed the 'Assessment for Learning Principles and Guidance' booklet which provided suggestions on how to meet the themes as well as providing existing examples of good practice.

On-going Socialization of the ESCAPE Work

An annual University of Hertfordshire Learning and Teaching conference was dedicated to assessment which included a key note address from the project director. Distributing coffee mugs imprinted with the ESACPE themes to all conference delegates.

Supporting New Faculty

New faculty are introduced to the University of Hertfordshire Curriculum Design Toolkit. One strand of which includes Assessment for Learning which was developed as part of the ESCAPE work. Components of the toolkit include Research Informed Principles of Good Practice, a self-diagnostic tool, Features and Consequences of practice, examples of how to improve practice (related to the Principles).

Making the Assessment Landscape Production Efficient

Within the University of Hertfordshire's Learning Management System (LMS), there now exists a bespoke tool that automatically creates Assessment Timelines and an Assessment Landscape. Doing so allows faculty and program teams to spend their effort on pedagogical discussions and designs rather than the production of a Landscape.

The display, can be filtered to show programs of study, levels of study and for faculty; all courses on which they teach (which may include courses across more than one program of study). Figure 4.5 shows the level 4 (first year) Assessment Landscape for BSc Molecular Biology. Hovering over the individual assignment deadline provides pop-up comments with brief details of the assignment type (Note the pop-up indicating a poster presentation.) Further details, including the assignment brief and learning outcomes being assessed, can be gained by clicking on the assignment deadline icon. Given that the Assessment Landscape is populated by information from the LMS' courses any minor changes to assignments within the courses (e.g. changes to the submission date) are instantly visible within the Landscape.

This digital Assessment Landscape enables program teams to easily see the assessment requirements across the courses, the types of assessments and the pressure points in relation to student and faculty effort. This is particularly useful for viewing programs with choice/optional courses (e.g. Joint Honour degree programs).

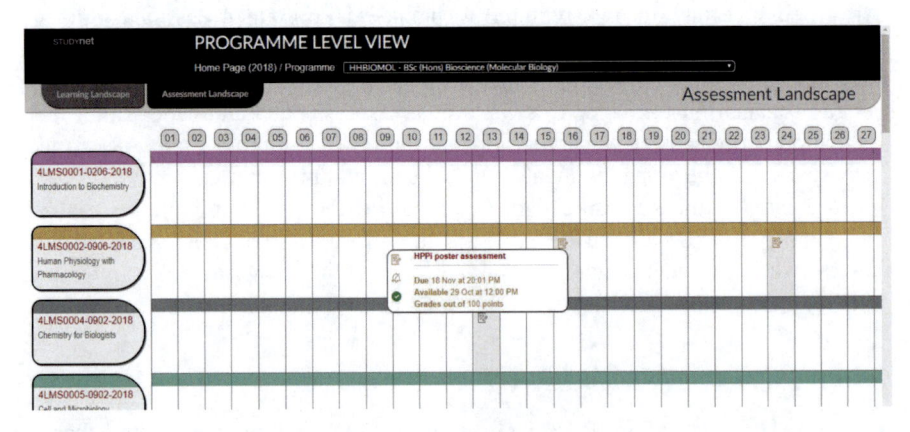

Figure 4.5. An example of an Assessment Landscape produced within the university's LMS

It is clear, that the tenets and tools of the ESCAPE Project still exist at the University of Hertfordshire due to the ways in which policy, technology developments, and curriculum enhancement have been considered and embedded. Such will help ensure the work creates an ongoing institution benefit long after the original project finished.

KING'S COLLEGE LONDON

During 2012 the ESCAPE Project Director moved to King's College London. Around that time, King's was also developing their interest in responding to their assessment challenges and tasked the ESCAPE Project Director to lead an initiative across the university. Following a workshop with the education leadership from each department, the project team (the Director and a dedicated Research Assistant) worked with 7 of the 9 Faculties, across 21 programs of study. The team mapped out the current assessment activity using the Assessment Landscape and the Assessment Mapping tools.

Motivations among departments for collaborating with the project varied from one to the next. Initially, strong direction was given from the Vice Principal (Education). Gradually departments applied to join the work, as they became aware of the benefits initial programs and departments were realizing, particularly in the use of the Assessment Landscapes in investigating and communicating the design and rationale of a programme of study and its component parts. Entrepreneurism played a part too; Faculty or department Vice Deans of Education, or new Program Directors, would engage with the project to inject good assessment and feedback practice into their developing pedagogy.

One of the partner departments developed a new program and paid specific attention to the programmatic assessment mapping from the ESCAPE Project and seeking to ensure that assessment linkages were made both within and across courses at the Program Design phase. The MSc. Genes, Environment & Development in Psychology & Psychiatry used the ESCAPE project's techniques into its curriculum, and with a process of ongoing validation and review, represents some of the most innovative assessment and feedback programmatic practice at King's.

As a large, multi-disciplinary institution, King's offered a chance to apply and develop the techniques from the ESCAPE project in areas ranging from English and Geography, through Law and Nursing to Pharmacology & Forensic Science. Addionally, the Project team were invited to run the Assessment and Feedback course in King's highly regarded Postgraduate Certificate in Academic Practice (PGCAP). The PGCAP is aimed (primarily) at new faculty and researchers at and beyond the university. The team incorporated into the course many of the ESCAPE tools; including the mapping of assessments across a program, plotting of assessment types with a view to comparing efficiency and fitness for purpose, and engaging program teams in exercises which would explore their own preconceptions and those of their students around assessment.

Indeed, the assessment task for delegates on the Course was to explore, using the ESCAPE tools, the assessment on a level of study and make genuine recommendations to their Head of Department. This real investigation prompted additional departmental discussions as well as socializing the tools to new faculty that would likely progress and take up responsibility for courses of study in the future. Doing so now creates other ESCAPE and assessment champions and will help sustain the work at King's.

The assessment mapping and creation of programmatic Assessment Landscapes spread beyond faculty and program teams at King's. The various visual representations of assessment are routinely used by many departments during student induction to:

- Show students the overarching assessment strategy/assessment diet.
- Reveal to students the timeline distribution of assessment.
- Identify to students how assessment tasks and the feedback from one task influences another assessment task.
- Develop the students' awareness of such terms as high-stakes, formative, summative and diagnostic assessment types.

All of which starts to help the assessment literacy of the incoming students.

As the work progressed at King's College London, the project team began to use the university's SharePoint tool to record data about assessment activities across a program using. Doing so also allowed for the auto creation of Assessment Landscapes and allowed the program team (and students) to see electronically the assessment activity of the course, level and program.

KHALIFA UNIVERSITY OF SCIENCE AND TECHNOLOGY

Towards the end of 2016, the ESCAPE Project Director left King's College London and joined Khalifa University of Science and Technology. In contrast to the University of Hertfordshire and King's College London, Khalifa University is a small and relatively new university located in the heart of Abu Dhabi. Khalifa University has firmly oriented itself as being research intensive and has programs of study mainly focused in the Science, Technology and Engineering disciplines.

Khalifa University's commitment to small class sizes (circa 30 students) creates opportunities for education to be personalized, dialogic and allow faculty and students to more readily develop an academic working relationship. Such are examples of good practice in undergraduate education as espoused by Chickering and Gamson (1987). One of the challenges with a desire for small classes however, is the need for multiple sections to be offered. i.e. for a class size of around 90, three sections (separate instances of the course) are needed. Whilst in some situations multiple sections might be taught the same faculty, it is possible (indeed likely), that different faculty will teach different sections of the same course. And whilst this brings the potential for faculty flair and individualism to flourish it also creates a potential for variability in assessment and student experience between the various sections.

Given this potential for variability, at Khalifa University we now intend to use the Assessment Landscaping tool to explore the:

- Core assessment components of the course and ensure they feature within each section.
- Assessment any variance that exist across the sections.
- Connections across courses (on the same year of study and across the various of years of study).

At Khalifa University a new line of inquiry will also be explored. This new line of inquiry will map the interconnectedness of assessment and feedback from student perspectives. The work to date (at the University of Hertfordshire and King's College London) has focused primarily on the assessment descriptions as set out in course and program handbooks and on the faculty's perspectives and articulations of the assessment connections. This new line of inquiry is likely to identify how well the formal documentation and the Faculty perspectives translate to the student experience.

SUMMARY

The challenge around student satisfaction, particularly in the assessment domain, is unlikely to diminish. This somewhat downbeat assertion should not detract faculty, program teams and institutions from their assessment/curriculum explorations and constantly reflecting on what and how we conceive and implement assessment. The use of the ESCAPE Project approach and tools, which seeks to deliberately create programmatic-and-socialized assessment designs has worked across cross different disciplinary groups and across different institution types. The approach and tools do not appear to hinder the so-called signature pedagogies of the disciplines but rather help to capture (visually) the program's assessment strategy and the operationalizing of such a strategy in a non-judgmental way. These visual-captures can then be explored with the program team to ensure the assessment is fit-for-purpose and is likely to help students develop the right set of attributes as their progress through the program.

Importantly, the work outlined above has shown that Projects, initially located within an institution, can successfully be migrated to other institutions and be further enhanced by the development of policy, faculty support and technological development. Such leads to diffusion of expertise and sustainability of the benefits.

REFERENCES

Anderson, I., Bullen, P., Alltree, J., & Thornton, H. (2008). CABLE an approach to embedding blended learning in the curricula and across the institution. *Reflecting Education, 4*(1), 30–41.

Biggs, J. B., & Tang, C. (2011). *Teaching for quality learning at university* (4th ed.). Maidenhead: McGraw Hill Education & Open University Press.

Chickering, A. W., & Gamson, Z. F. (1987). Seven principles for good practice in undergraduate education. *AAHE Bulletin*, 3–7.

Gibbs, G., & Simpson, C. (2004). Conditions under which assessment supports student learning. *Learning and Teaching in Higher Education, 1*, 3–31.

Higher Education Funding Council for England (HEFCE). (2017). *Unistats data set*. Retrieved March 2, 2018, from http://www.hefce.ac.uk/lt/unikis/

Miller, C. M. L., & Parlett, M. (1974). *Up to the mark: A study of the examination game*. London: Society for Research into Higher Education.

Nicol, D., & Macfarlane-Dick, D. (2006). Formative assessment and self-regulated learning: A model and seven principles of good feedback practice. *Studies in Higher Education, 31*(2), 199–218.

QAA. (2018). *The UK quality code for higher education*. Retrieved March 2, 2018, from http://www.qaa.ac.uk/assuring-standards-and-quality/the-quality-code

Russell, M. B, Barefoot, H., & Bygate, D. (2013). Making learning-oriented assessment the experience of all our students: Supporting institutional change. In S. Merry, M. Price, D. Carless, & M. Taras (Eds.), *Reconceptualising feedback in higher education: Developing dialogue with students*. Oxon: Routledge.

Russell, M. B., & Bygate, D. (2010). Assessment for learning: An introduction to the ESCAPE project. *Blended Learning in Practice*, 38–48.

Salmon, G. (2015). *Carpe diem planning process handbook*. Retrieved March 2, 2018, from http://www.gillysalmon.com/uploads/1/6/0/5/16055858/carpe_diem_planning_process_workbook_v17-january_2015.pdf

Seeto, D., & Vlachopoulos, P. (2015). *Design develop implement: A team based approach to learning design*. Paper presented at the THETA 2015 Conference, Gold Coast, Australia.

Snyder, B. (1971). *The hidden curriculum*. New York, NY: Alfred A. Knop.

Mark Russell
Khalifa University of Science and Technology
United Arab Emirates

Helen Barefoot
University of Hertfordshire
United Kingdom

Bryan Taylor
University College London
United Kingdom

Leigh Powell
Khalifa University of Science and Technology
United Arab Emirates

DON KLINGER

5. THE PITFALLS AND POTENTIALS OF CLASSROOM AND LARGE-SCALE ASSESSMENTS

INTRODUCTION

My entry to the world of classroom and large-scale assessment began in the late 1980s when I completed my degree to become an educator and subsequently when I started to work as a high-school teacher in Canada. The province of British Columbia, had recently introduced high-stakes provincial examinations for Grade 12 (final year) academic courses. These examinations contributed 40% to students' grades and universities were beginning to use these course grades as determinants for university entrance. Further, schools were increasingly being evaluated and ranked based on student performance across these provincial examinations. In essence, these testing programs had grown in use to serve the purposes of "achievement, accountability, and admissions" and this trend towards expanded use has long since continued (e.g., Klinger, 2002; Klinger, DeLuca, & Miller, 2008; Nagy, 2000).

As an initial teacher, I became concerned about the impact these external examinations would have on classroom teaching and assessment, something that has long since been demonstrated (e.g., Darling-Hammond, Ancess, & Falk, 1994; Polesel, Rice, & Dulfer, 2013; Popham, 2002; Shepard, 1991). Nevertheless, as I began my own educational journey, I also observed the potential of these large-scale assessments to provide a reasonable external measure of students' learning, and a focus on the key concepts for my own classroom teaching. I did not want these assessments to get in the way of teaching and I did not want the provincial tests to be the focal point of my teaching. Hence I began to explore my own classroom teaching and assessment practices, with the intent of minimising the time devoted to formal assessments (e.g., tests) and grading students' work. I soon discovered a variety of instructional and assessment practices in which the students took on much of the responsibility for monitoring their own learning. It reduced my assessment workload and my students' learning seemed to also increase, and this was shown to extend to the provincial testing results for the students, as their results reached heights not attained in the school beforehand.

These initial experiences as a teacher shaped the focus of my previous and ongoing research. As a professor and researcher, I have continually explored both classroom and large-scale assessment. I have grown to deeply appreciate the role that both can play in the service of education. Concurrently, I have witnessed the misuse and misinformation about teaching, learning, and assessment. For example, there is much promotion about learning styles, gender differences that impact learning, or the value of diagnostic testing in the classroom. Yet the vast majority of these ideas have yet to withstand the scrutiny of empirical research. Similarly, formative assessment and "Assessment for Learning" (AfL) have been lauded as panaceas for improving student achievement (e.g., Black, Harrison, & Lee, 2003; Wiliam, 2011). In contrast, external large-scale assessments have been almost universally blamed for negatively impacting both teaching and learning.

The truth is much more tempered and nuanced than what is contained in the bold claims, criticisms, rhetoric and promotion. Hence I present my current perspectives on classroom and large-scale assessment, based on my ongoing collaborative research, and the work of others who are continuing to work to support and understand teaching and learning across educational jurisdictions. I intend to highlight some of the disagreements and ongoing academic debates occurring in the field of educational measurement and assessment, while also acknowledging the opportunities both classroom and large-scale assessment provide to enhance both teaching and learning. Throughout, my intention is to demonstrate the importance of thoughtful implementation of assessment practices and the need for ongoing critical reflection of our current assessment practices and the current plans for future educational directions and policies related to assessment.

STUDENT ASSESSMENT IN THE CLASSROOM

The classroom teacher is central to shaping and directing the learning experiences of students. While the central role of instruction and directing learning is beyond debate, the teacher's role in determining student achievement has not yet been universally accepted. There continue to be many examples in which external examinations are used as the sole determinant or a major contributor to a student's grade, especially in the later grades in which such decisions have more important stakes for subsequent learning opportunities. Even in the earlier grades, teachers' classroom assessment practices are often complemented with some form of external assessments, used for either diagnostic or summative purposes. Within such diversity of the role of external and large-scale assessments, it is not at all surprising that teachers' classroom assessment practices have developed and evolved into a myriad of practices and purposes.

I argue that the classroom assessment practices of teachers have traditionally served to first to measure students' learning, and to a lesser extent, guide instruction. These traditional purposes can be broadly categorized into three domains: (1) measure student achievement across a learning domain; (2) determine individual student competence; and (3) inform and direct teaching practice. Certainly, these purposes have been and remain appropriate, albeit with caveats. In terms of measuring student achievement across a learning domain, teachers have been shown to be able to broadly separate and sort their students in terms of overall achievement. This has and still largely occurs within a norm-referenced framework, demonstrating that teachers are able to recognize the differences in the quality of students' work and achievement. Critical to meeting this purpose is time and multiple assessments, since teacher developed assessments, while expected to be closely linked to relevant learning activities, are generally lacking in quality (e.g., reliability).

Second, the use of classroom assessment to determine individual student competence reflects an evolution of the purpose described above from norm- to criterion-referenced assessment and grading. Criterion-referenced classroom assessment practices are superior measures of student achievement and learning in comparison to the more traditional norm-referenced systems that were previously used; however, such practices require well-defined performance standards and/or rubrics. As someone who has worked for many years with teachers as they learn to create and articulate such standard, I can attest to the difficulty teachers face in developing these skills. (see also, Popham, 1997). As a result, the shift from norm- to criterion-referenced assessment practices has been very slow as teachers continue to struggle to define competence.

It was not long after Scriven (1967) introduced the term formative evaluation that it moved from program evaluation to include classroom assessment (Bloom, Hastings, & Madaus, 1971). Key to this early conception of formative assessment was the use of assessment practices and results to inform and direct teaching practice. While students were actively engaged in the assessment itself, they were very passive users of the assessment information. Effective formative assessment in the classroom requires teachers to purposely develop and enact assessments to accurately monitor students' mastery of the learning expectations. Teachers must use formative practices that provide fast, reliable and accurate information to direct subsequent teaching. And this attention and work needs to occur before, during and after the assessment process.

Teachers' classroom assessment activities have been subjected to a long history of research and review. I continue to work with teachers to enhance their classroom assessment skills, and much of my work has focused on developing foundational assessment skills (Klinger, McDivitt, Howard, Rogers, Wylie, & Munoz, 2015). These include technical skills related to the development of high quality assessment tasks and methods to more accurately evaluate individual student achievement and competence. One of the primary and initial challenges for teachers is to hep them identify their own assessment biases. As examples, these biases may arise with the selection of the assessment practices to be used or through a teacher's unrealized biases towards their students, which may result in either the under-or over-estimation of an individual student's learning. Second, even though most teachers lack adequate training, they have an inherent faith in the comparability of their assessment practices. Without well-defined performance standards, or complex equating procedures, such assessments are rarely if ever comparable.

More recent trends have put even further pressure on the need for high-quality classroom assessment. Specifically, within the reasonable recognition of the value of classroom assessment, there has been an increasing, and much less reasonable, focus on using classroom assessment results as a measure of teaching effectiveness and accountability. These classroom assessment results then become measures to demonstrate attainment of school improvement targets. Simply stated, this is a dangerous trend, and needs great caution. Similarly, there has been an even more recent trend for teachers to use pre-tests and post-tests as a diagnostic tool. Once again, this has created a dangerous trend, in which teachers are now conducting formal assessments prior to teaching, with the intention of demonstrating that subsequent teaching will improve achievement. In an attempt to mimic research designs, these teachers are forsaking teaching and learning time. Further, these assessments rarely have the specificity to accurately inform teaching. The result is time lost to a weak assessment process that will have minimal impact on improving teaching or learning.

Perhaps the biggest shifts in classroom assessment are occurring in relationship to formative assessment (e.g., Black & Wiliam, 1998, 2003; Wiliam, Lee, Harrison, & Black, 2004). And this was certainly a critical foundation for our work with the Joint Committee on Standards for Educational Evaluation (JCSEE) to develop the Classroom Assessment Standards (Klinger et al., 2016). There is a body of research that "suggests that well structured formative assessment and feedback supports learning and increases students' abilities to monitor their own learning" (Klinger, 2017; see also Nicol & Macfarlane-Dick, 2006). Often framed under the heading of "Assessment for Learning" (AfL), the central tenet of AfL is the shift from formative assessment being a resource for teachers to one in which students transition from the role of passive receiver of assessment information to to engaged learner and user of assessment information. While several terms have been used to describe this active student process, for example, "Assessment As Learning" (AaL), executive functioning, or meta-cognition, self-regulated learning tends to be the most commonly used and referenced concept (e.g., Nicol & Macfarlane-Dick, 2006). There is no doubt that such formative assessment practices have the potential to deeply engage students in their learning, and can be an highly effective teaching and learning support that increases achievement and other important educational outcomes for students.

These are laudable goals for classroom assessment but they underlie a complex process of learning and implementation for both teachers and students. My ongoing research with colleagues and educators has highlighted a series of teaching, learning, and assessment processes that appear to enhance students' self-regulation skills and support more effective classroom assessment practices (DeLuca, Klinger, Chapman, & LaPointe McEwan, 2017; DeLuca, Klinger, Pyper, & Woods, 2015; Klinger, Volante, & DeLuca, 2012). First, educators must teach, model, promote, and perhaps even measure the critical aspects of self-regulated learning. Students will not develop such skills without explicit teaching and practice. Second, teachers and students need to not only understand, but also create a learning environment in which instruction, learning and assessment are integrated parts of the "learning experience". Related to this is a classroom environment in which students and teachers both have active roles in the assessment experience, before, during, and after instruction. This requires teachers to release some of the responsibility and control they have typically held within their classrooms. This release of responsibilities can only occur if the first two processes are in place.

Lastly, the effectiveness of classroom assessment practices to support teaching and learning are based on the quality of the feedback these assessments can provide (e.g., Hattie, 2013; Hattie & Timperley, 2007). Teachers are comfortable providing quick encouraging comments, for example, "Good work", "You are getting there", "Good effort", etc. Unfortunately, these forms of feedback do little to support teaching or learning (Brookhart, 1999, 2017). Yet, these forms of practice continue to be dominant in our classrooms. Teaching and learning requires more focused feedback and this feedback needs to be linked to learning expectations and descriptive, providing specific strengths, weaknesses, and next steps. This brings me back to the earlier discussion on rubrics. While challenging to develop, effective rubrics can be a powerful method for teachers to provide directive feedback to students. Further, students can use these rubrics to monitor and direct their own learning, enhancing self-regulation.

Critical to the value of feedback within the classroom is the shift from such feedback to be a transmissive process from the teacher to the student to one in which the feedback becomes a dialogue, and this dialogue can occur between the teacher and the student, student to student (peer), and even an internal, individual student dialogue (self). While there is strong support for the use of feedback, our recent work with teachers and colleagues has led to a shift in the language we are using to describe these assessment activities, moving from feedback to "assessment dialogues" to what I now term a "learning dialogue". Furthering the previous research and literature (e.g., Brookhart, 1999, 2017; Hattie, 2013), such learning dialogues have the potential to integrate teaching, learning and assessment, enhancing students' learning outcomes, and self-regulation abilities.

EXTERNAL METHODS OF STUDENT ASSESSMENT

As the concept of schooling extended to include larger portions of the population, the need for more "objective" measures of achievement also grew. The history of such external forms of assessment can be traced back over 2000 years to China (Cheng, 2009). However, their use in relation to schooling has a much shorter history. Admittedly, my educational work has occurred largely in the Canadian context. Hence my overview of the purposes, challenges and potentials of large-scale testing is largely based on the Canadian experience (Klinger, 2002, 2016; Klinger et al., 2008; Klinger, Maggi, & D'Angiulli, 2011). Nevertheless, there are parallels with the experiences of other educational jurisdictions.

As with classroom assessment, large-scale assessments have been used for a variety of purposes, ranging from measuring student achievement within both low- and high-stakes testing environments, to system monitoring and accountability to decisions regarding access to educational programs or opportunities. I contend that large-scale assessment practices can be broadly categorized into three domains: (1) broadly determine student achievement across a defined domain; (2) inform educational policy and direction; and (3) provide a reliable measure of individual achievement within a reduced domain. Without doubt, these broad purposes are likely appropriate in a variety of contexts albeit with their own set of caveats.

Perhaps one of the most common purposes of large-scale testing is related to efforts to broadly determine student achievement across a defined domain. It is within this context that examination programs such as PISA, TIMMS, PIRLS, and other international assessment programs operate (e.g., O'Grady, Deussing, Scerbina, Fung, & Muhe, 2016). Within national contexts, this same purpose is used in many of the low-stakes testing programs found across Canada and in other international, educational jurisdictions (Klinger et al., 2008). Given that these assessments are generally administered, at best, on an annual basis, they only provide a single measure in time. Hence their use requires careful attention to psychometric quality and administration to provide useful information.

Related to this first broad purpose, is the use of large-scale assessments to inform educational policy and direction. Most commonly, these purposes are related to measures used for system monitoring and accountability or as a data source for school improvement efforts. Caution must be exercised as such assessment programs tend to cover a relatively broad domain. Thus, while such assessments may identify broad areas for policy direction, they rarely provide sufficient information for specific practices or policies to be enacted. Lastly, large-scale testing programs are commonly used to measure individual achievement. Such assessments may occur within either a low-stakes system in which the results have very little explicit consequences for students, or within a high-stakes system in which students' performance have much higher consequences for individual students. As described earlier, the results for these tests may be used to determine students' grades, be a requirement for graduation, or be used in admission decisions. The technical quality of large-scale tests in terms of item characteristics and reliability is usually very high. Nevertheless, the manner in which these tests are to be used, and the common single administration of such tests, results in a narrower domain for testing and a need for validity evidence, an aspect that typically receives too little attention.

Unlike many critics, I support the thoughtful use of large-scale testing programs. Well constructed tests can and have been shown to defensibly serve the three broad purposes above. My concerns regarding the current and "planned" uses for large-scale testing lies within the ongoing attempts to further expand the role of these tests, with little attention to the validity of such purposes. Foremost amongst these concerns and what I would call "Pitfalls" is the ongoing use of such tests for the purposes of evaluating the effectiveness of educational interventions, whether they are at the classroom, school, or national level. Without early attention to such a purpose in the design and development phase, these assessments have been found to be surprisingly insensitive to specific interventions to modify students' learning.

This should not be surprising given that most successful interventions are targeted towards a very specific learning expectation or student population, and these tests are, by design, focused on much broader educational outcomes. Ongoing evidence of this lack of fit is observed in the common pattern of change observed with the introduction a testing program. Initially, test results show an increasing trend over the first few iterations. Over a relatively short period of time (under 5 years), the results tend to level off and become extremely resistant to further efforts to improve student achievement. I argue that these first few years are a result of teachers' efforts to incorporate and align some of the testing practices into their own teaching, creating familiarity with the test and a closer teaching/testing alignment. This alignment may be very appropriate if it focuses on the constructs to be taught and tested rather than the test design. Nevertheless, further improvement may be too subtle or focused to be measured by the broader domain measured by the tests.

Related to this first pitfall, I have grown weary of the argument that testing should be a driver of educational change. Far too often I have heard the phrase, "What gets measured gets valued". I tend to now respond with this quote, which has been attributed to many people (e.g., Cameron, Deming, Eisner, Einstein) with a variety of similar wordings: "Not everything that matters can be measured, and not everything that is measured matters". My point is that large-scale testing should not be used as the primary focus for educational reform and change. The driver for change should be a thoughtful analysis of what is needed to best prepare our children for success in their educational journey and future lives. Once this has been established, conversations could then begin with measurement specialists to determine the extent to which appropriate measures can or cannot be implemented. As a recent example, I fear for the success of the current debate around 21st Century learning skills. While I, along with many others, argue these are long standing desired skills, the current focus on developing measures of these skills rather than the teaching and learning of these skills is highly misinformed at best.

Lastly, the unabated use of such testing programs for high-stakes decisions continues. Student performance on such testing programs has long been used as a "contributor" to the determination of their individual success; however, there are far too many examples of these tests being the sole "determiner" of a student's' achievement or competency. As noted above, the technical quality of these tests meet a very high standard. Yet the lack of breadth of domain coverage of these tests and the singular administration narrow the construct and context being examined, and thus provide an incomplete measure of what is being measured. Ultimately, these tests do not adequately acknowledge the impact of educational and student contexts.

"Research continually identifies factors that are associated with differences in student achievement on large-scale examinations. These factors are likely to be "Differences that Matter" and we have found student-, teacher-, and school-level predictors of student achievement" (Klinger, 2017). Much of my work has focused on predictors of student achievement using large-scale tests as the outcome measure. In spite of the limitations described above, these studies have provided important findings not only in my research but also in the research of others. We do know that the vast majority to differences in student achievement can be attributed to student level factors. These include socio-economic background, parental education, student mobility, identified learning needs, reading practices, and a host of others we have yet to fully identify.

Fortunately, we have found that there are also differences in student learning that can be attributed to teachers and schools. This means that some teachers and schools are more effective at helping students attain measured educational outcomes than others. Content knowledge, when subjects are taught, teacher gender, discipline climate, school location and school size (bigger is better), have all been associated with increased student performance. Of course, the caution here is that these factors have largely yet to be demonstrated to have causal links to student achievement and they may not be consistent across curriculum or jurisdictions.

If large-scale testing efforts are to meet their goals, we must first acknowledge the limitations of these assessments. We must always clearly define the purposes of assessments in use or planned to be used. These purposes will then inform the development, implementation, scoring, and subsequent use of the results. There are no shortcuts. We need to take the time for quality development. This attention to quality control occurs before, during and long after implementation of testing programs. I am a strong defender of large-scale educational assessment programs and there is ongoing evidence that these assessments provide system valuable feedback. Yet, as I previously argued with respect to classroom assessment, it is the opportunities to start valuable "learning dialogues" that may be most beneficial, especially if these dialogues occur amongst educators, researchers and policy makers.

MOVING FORWARD

Those involved in assessment and measurement research have certainly been witness to the growing importance of both classroom and large-scale assessment. This is not a debate regarding the superiority of one form over the other. Rather, we need to continue to focus on the roles that each plays in supporting education. Unfortunately, this has been a surprisingly challenging debate, and there has certainly been a conflation of purposes between classroom and large-scale assessment. It is not my intention to argue against the current or evolving purposes and uses of educational assessment. My critiques rest with the increasingly unexamined purposes of assessment. There may be very appropriate new purposes that can be met with both classroom assessment and large-scale assessment programs; however, these purposes cannot simply be a result of an untested decision or statement for such use.

As an example, the International Association for the Evaluation of Educational Achievement (IEA, 2016) stated that their testing programs such as TIMMS can be used to "make informed decisions about how to improve teaching and learning". Similarly, Alberta Education (n.d.) states that its Provincial Achievement Tests can be used to "determine if students are learning what they are expected to learn"

(Alberta Education, n.d.). These are untested assumptions. As I have stated above, the implied specificity of these goals appears to be beyond the abilities of current large-scale testing programs for the foreseeable future. A similar situation can be observed with PISA. Its global comparison of educational jurisdictions has become a lightning rod for educational policy makers and governments for educational reform. While I cannot speak to this with respect to other jurisdictions, there is almost a complete lack of familiarity or impact of PISA amongst teachers in Canada.

A further disturbing conflation of purpose has been the recent trend to use large-scale testing programs for formative assessment purposes. Once again, there is little current evidence that such uses are appropriate or informative. Similar conflation can be observed with classroom assessments as they are being used as sources of data for school improvement efforts and "teacher- and school-based" inquiry into the effectiveness of their improvement efforts.

In order to look forward, it is important to first understand what is behind these shifts in educational assessment in which classroom and large scale assessment are being tasked with increasingly important roles in supporting teaching and learning while also playing important roles in grading and system monitoring. I want to highlight some of the education and challenges we are facing that may be exerting pressure on these decisions and purposes.

First, our classrooms look different today than at any other time, and the classroom is a complex environment. There is a greater integration of students with special education needs. Migration patterns have resulted in highly diverse classroom environments, both culturally and economically. As a result, teachers must work differently to meet the educational needs of an increasingly diverse student population. And these students often have very different levels of access to educational resources and supports. All this is occurring during a time in which education, as a critical societal enterprise, is under ongoing and increasing scrutiny. Further, the scope of responsibility for educators and education as a whole is increasing to now include physical and mental health and well-being, 21st century learning skills, and increasingly complex competencies. The changing expectations for classroom assessment practices further highlight this growing complexity as teachers must monitor students' success at attaining increasingly complex knowledge and skills. At the same time, teachers must help students become more independent, self-regulated learners who are able to monitor personal strengths and weaknesses and set short- and long-term learning goals. I work with highly skilled professionals and this is a daunting task for them, let alone for our children.

With the acknowledgement of the complexity of today's classrooms, learning outcomes and competencies to be learned, and evolving assessment practices, our path forward must be one of patience. Much of my research and work has been with pre-service and practicing teachers (e.g., Cooper, Klinger, & McAdie, 2017; DeLuca et al., 2015; Klinger et al., 2012; LaPointe-McEwan, DeLuca, & Klinger, 2017). Common across this work has been the need for specific teacher training and learning, and this requires time; time to learn and time to practice (e.g., LaPointe, Klinger, Billen, & Newman, 2017). We need to acknowledge that complex learning will not occur quickly, and that both teachers and systems need to have permission to "make mistakes" as we navigate this learning and implementation. Second, this learning requires a much better integration of quality research and knowledge, presented in a manner that explicitly highlights the implications of the research for teaching and assessment practices (Cooper et al., 2017).

A necessary result of these efforts will be the evolution of thoughtful criticality and support. This will have the benefit of reducing the rhetoric and untested assumptions of assessment debates and efforts. Lastly, and without minimising our collective efforts, we need to be honest. I have had the pleasure and honour to work with assessment and measurement researchers, policy makers, and educators. Universally, they are all committed to quality education and learning. Yet these shared desires are often lost in tine issues and debates I have explored here. I have no doubt that honest reflection and acknowledgement of issues, challenges, and potential would go far to move assessment practices, both in the classroom and in large-scale testing programs, forward.

REFERENCES

Alberta Education. (2018). *About the PATs*. Retrieved March 17, 2018, from https://education.alberta.ca/provincial-achievement-tests/about-the-pats/

Black, P. J., Harrison, C., & Lee, C. (2003). *Assessment for learning: Putting it into practice*. Berkshire: McGraw-Hill Education.

Black, P. J., & Wiliam, D. (1998). Assessment and classroom learning. *Assessment in Education: Principles Policy and Practice, 5*(1), 7–73.

Black, P. J., & Wiliam, D. (2003). In praise of educational research: Formative assessment. *British Educational Research Journal, 29*(5), 623–637.

Bloom, B. S., Hastings, J. T., & Madaus, G. F. (Eds.). (1971). *Handbook on the formative and summative evaluation of student learning*. New York, NY: McGraw-Hill.

Brookhart, S. M. (1999). Teaching about communicating assessment results and grading. *Educational Measurement: Issues and Practice, 18*(1), 5–13.

Brookhart, S. M. (2017). *How to give effective feedback to your students* (2nd ed.). Alexandria, VA: Association for Supervision and Curriculum Development.

Cheng, L. (2008). The key to success: English language testing in China. *Language Testing, 25*(1), 15–37.

Cooper, A., Klinger, D. A., & McAdie, P. (2017). What do teachers need? An exploration of evidence-informed practice for classroom assessment in Ontario. *Educational Research. Special Issue: Evidence-informed Practice in Education, 59*(2), 190–208.

Darling-Hammond, L., Ancess, J., & Falk, B. (1994). *Authentic assessment in action: Studies of schools and Students at work*. New York, NY: Teachers College Press.

DeLuca, C., Klinger, D. A., Chapman, A., & LaPointe-McEwan, D. (2017). Student perspectives on assessment for learning. *The Curriculum Journal, 29*(1), 77–94.

DeLuca, C., Klinger, D. A., Pyper, J., & Woods, J. (2015). Instructional rounds as a professional learning model for systemic implementation of assessment for learning. *Assessment in Education: Principles, Policy and Practice, 22*(1), 122–139. (online first 23 October 2014)

Hattie, J. (2013). *Visible learning: A synthesis of over 800 meta-analyses relating to achievement*. New York, NY: Routledge.

Hattie, J., & Timperley, H. (2007). The power of feedback. *Review of Educational Research, 77*(1), 81–112.

International Association for the Evaluation of Educational Achievement. (2016). *TIMMS & PIRLS: About TIMMS 2015*. Retrieved March 17, 2018, from http://timss2015.org/timss-2015/about-timss-2015/

Klinger, D. A. (2002). Oops, that was a mistake: Examining the effects and implications of changing assessment policies. In P. deBrouker & A. Sweetman (Eds.), *Towards evidence-based policy for Canadian education* (pp. 333–346). Montreal & Kingston: McGill-Queen's University Press.

Klinger, D. A. (2016). Monitoring accountability, and improvement, oh no! Assessment policies and practices in Canadian education. In S. Scott, D. E. Scott, & C. F. Webber (Eds.), *Assessment in education: Implications for leadership* (pp. 53–65). Switzerland: Springer.

Klinger, D. A. (2017, November 5–6). *The potentials and pitfalls of classroom and large scale assessments.* Invited Keynote Speaker at the 1st International Conference on Educational Measurement, Evaluation and Assessment, Abu Dhabi, United Arab Emirates.

Klinger, D. A., DeLuca, C., & Miller, T. (2008). The evolving culture of large-scale assessments in Canadian education. *Canadian Journal of Educational Administration and Policy, 76*(1), 1–34. Retrieved from http://www.umanitoba.ca/publications/cjeap/articles/klinger.html

Klinger, D. A., Maggi, S., & D'Angiulli, A. (2011). School accountability and assessment: Should we put the roof up first. *The Educational Forum, 75*(2), 114–128.

Klinger, D. A., Volante, L., & DeLuca, C. (2012). Building teacher capacity within the evolving assessment culture in Canadian education. *Policy Futures in Education, Special Edition: Developing Sustainable Assessment Cultures in School Learning Organisations, 10*, 447–460.

LaPointe, D., Klinger, D. A., Billen, T., & Newman, E. (2017). *Collaborative developmental evaluation report for the eastern Ontario staff development network mathematics project year 4.* Kingston: Queen's University, Faculty of Education.

LaPointe-McEwan, D., DeLuca, C., & Klinger, D. A. (2017). Supporting evidence-use in networked professional learning: The role of the middle leader. *Educational Research: Special Issue: Evidence-informed Practice in Education, 59*(2) 136–153.

Nagy, P. (2000). The Three roles of assessment: Gatekeeping, accountability, and instructional diagnosis. *Canadian Journal of Education, 25*(4), 262–279.

Nicol, D. J., & Macfarlane-Dick, D. (2006). Formative assessment and self-regulated learning: A model and seven principles of good feedback practice. *Studies in Higher Education, 31*(2), 199–218.

O'Grady, K., Deussing, M., Scerbina, T., Fung, K., & Muhe, N. (2016). *Measuring up: Canadian results of the OECD PISA study. The performance of Canada's youth in science, reading and mathematics: 2015 first results for Canadians aged 15.* Toronto: Council of Ministers of Education, Canada.

Polesel, J., Rice, S., & Dulfer, N. (2013). The impact of high-stakes testing on curriculum and pedagogy: A teacher perspective. *Australia Journal of Education Policy, 29*, 640–657. doi:10.1080/02680939.2013.865082

Popham, W. J. (1997). What's wrong – and what's right – with rubrics. *Educational Leadership, 55*(2), 72–75.

Popham, W. J. (2002). *High-stakes tests: Harmful, permanent, fixable.* Paper presented at the Annual Conference of the American Research Council, New Orleans, LO.

Scriven, M. (1967). *The methodology of evaluation.* Washington, DC: American Educational Research Association.

Shepard, L. A. (1991). Psychometrician's beliefs about learning. *Educational Researcher, 20*(6), 2–16.

Wiliam, D. (2011). What is assessment for learning? *Studies in Educational Evaluation, 37*(1), 3–14. doi:10.1016/j.stueduc.2011.03.001

Wiliam, D., Lee, C., Harrison, C., & Black, P. (2004). Teachers developing assessment for learning: Impact on student learning. *Assessment in Education, 11*(1), 49–65.

Don Klinger
University of Waikato
Hamilton, New Zealand

PATRICK GRIFFIN AND NAFISA AWWAL

6. A PROCESS PERSPECTIVE OF COLLABORATIVE PROBLEM SOLVING

INTRODUCTION

Over the past 20 to 30 years technology has become embedded in education in a manner almost as familiar as a textbook, the whiteboard, desks and pencil and paper. We continue to search for ways to respond to and identify social and cognitive skills that students are expected to develop to enable constructive living in a C21 global context. We are variously affected by a series of industrial revolutions and the tensions arising from the pressure to change when conservatism would have social structures retained. These pressures are felt in every household, classroom and workplace. In response we may need to explore the implications of social roles of education as either social reconstruction or social reproduction.

Curriculum from a social reproduction perspective is expected to help students to become citizens capable of functioning responsibly in an existing society. It aims to reproduce and sustain the status quo. A premise of a social reproduction curriculum is that it is not the role of education to critique society. Education in that paradigm is expected to provide information and skills necessary for the student to function well in an existing society. Social reproduction can have the effect of reducing teachers to become specialised technicians whose role it is to implement and manage the curriculum rather than develop the students as critical and competent members of society. The skilled technician teacher helps to perpetuate the implementation of the social reproduction curriculum which is based on content which the teacher transmits, and the students absorb. This is not the case in a competence model of education such as would be expected in contexts where problem solving, critical thinking and collaborative competencies are expected to be evident and to flourish.

Competency-based education represents a paradigm change a teacher's role from a transmissive to a transformative one. The scope and focus of the competence focused education will, in many societies, be controversial. Social reconstruction is diametrically opposed to social reproduction and the role of the teacher falls into two fundamentally different paradigms.

A competence approach to education involves active participation by 'doing'. It involves being able to monitor what students do, say, make or write as evidence of development. The 'doing (say, make or write)' is not drill and practice, or even completion of specific projects that the students define. In a competence model the school becomes a community to help the students develop attitudes, values and habits useful in improving the community. The competencies they develop must be interrelated. Separating one from another may be difficult given the infusion of social, ethical, aspirational competencies as well as skills in the overall competence performance.

Priorities need to be established and then a strategy is needed to ensure that the competencies are embedded in learning and teaching. Hence it may be more important to understand the process of competence demonstration and development rather than an outcome dichotomy of success or failure. The latter is characteristic of an industrial era of education and a content based curriculum feeding a social reproduction role. A competency focused curriculum emphasises quality of performance and leads to a reconstruction role. The two paradigms of education roles contradict each other in ways that are irreconcilable.

In a content based curriculum the teacher is expected to be a skilled technician; in the a competence focused social reconstructive curriculum the teacher is expected to be an autonomous transformative collaborator. Social reproduction and social reconstruction in education cannot coexist. These roles are alternatives, not supplementary. Hence systems of education must make a choice. Does the system move to a competence model with the aim of preparing society to live in aftermath of the fourth industrial revolution where intelligent machines are replacing human skills or does it continue with a reproductive approach with the goal of maintaining the status quo?

ATC21S

It is within this context that the project known as the ATC21S emerged in 2008. Three large digital corporations, Cisco, Intel and Microsoft were concerned that education was not changing commensurate with the pace of change in the workplace. Their "Call to Action" led to an exploratory workshop attended by than 250 researchers and industrialists in 2009 with the aim of exploring the needs of education in a C21, post-industrial context. The group defined the issues in terms of new ways of working, new tools for working, new ways of thinking and living in a digital world. By 2015, several global organisations such as the World Economic Forum, the Economist, the New York Academy of Sciences, European Network of Schools, International Labour Organisation, UNESCO, and the OECD all became actively engaged in the search for new directions in education that would enable schools to prepare citizens for a new and constantly changing society.

Several key ideas were common and constant across almost every analysis. The emphasis was placed on the development of competencies such as critical thinking, problem-solving, collaboration, creativity, and communication. It also became clear that citizens had to become increasingly familiar with scientific thinking, use of technology, coding and engineering of ideas and absolute mandatory were the development of communication competencies and application of mathematics.

Assessment specialists and psychometricians (whose traditional paper and pencil, multiple-choice, objectively scored test instruments were becoming obsolete) also struggled to find ways of measuring these new and supplementary competencies that would emphasise what people did, what they said, what they made or built or what they did with what they knew. An era of directly observable evidence quietly slipped in to the education context requiring direct evidence of what people do, say, make or write rather than the inferences of what they know, understand, think, believe or feel. The former is evidence, the latter inference. Along with the change of competence and content came a pressure to change assessment to make it primarily evidence-based rather than the traditional inference approach.

The three corporations set out to influence education systems and governments to examine new ways of testing, new ways of teaching, new ways of learning, new materials and techniques and technology to support these new shifts in education. In a meeting in late 2009 amongst a group of people working with the three corporations it was decided that the combination of collaboration, critical thinking, communication and problem solving could build on previous work on collaborative learning and in particular, computer-assisted collaborative learning to devise, construct, teach and measure a phenomenon called collaborative problem-solving. Such is the pace of change in education that the OECD took on board the idea of collaborative problem-solving and measured student competence in this field in 53 countries during 2015. The results were released in November 2017. While countries were interested, the report has not sparked a great deal of interest compared to the discussion that surrounds basic literacy and numeracy. Collaboration and problem solving, which are consistently described as critical for a post-industrial society dependent on the social reconstruction of education, barely raises a whimper. More surprising than the lack of interest, was the almost uncritical acceptance of the definition, the metric, or the procedures used to measure the competence.

For the ATC21S project, the work on collaborative problem-solving began by defining the construct and then building tasks that would enable students working collaboratively to solve a task-based problem. Given the nature of the sponsoring companies is not surprising that the first foray into this work would be digital, computer oriented, and Internet focused. Also given the power of technology the decision was also made that machine learning and artificial intelligence could assist the scoring and an understanding of how students were learning in solving problems collaboratively.

Three volumes of research papers have emerged from this project all published by Springer. Separately, a group of 30 researchers prepared a white paper for the United States government considering the introduction of collaborative problem solving into the National Assessment of Education Progress in the following 2 to 3 years. Countries including Singapore, Australia, Costa Rica, the Netherlands, Finland and the United States all participated in the ATC21S project and embraced the notion of changing their assessment to develop more efficient ways of measuring this new phenomenon.

The Education Testing Service in Princeton New Jersey established a research fund to investigate the construct. Countries such as Argentina and 11 Latin American countries have taken to studying students' thinking and collaboration skills as part of the curriculum. There is no doubt that education is changing, that assessment is changing and the technology of this is almost an unstoppable force for the future. The tasks in the ATC21S project assisted the search for data that would describe how students solved problems collaboratively – not whether they succeeded or failed in solving the problem but how they went about the resolution of the issue.

In order to address this, it was necessary to get data about the process followed in pursuing the resolution of the goal. The search opened a few new doors to the field of measurement and assessment and there is now a thriving research base around the world which is published in the third volume of the project (Care, Griffin, & Wilson, 2017). The first efforts were apparently successful and could have stopped there, but it did not. The lingering doubts about method, metric and analyses led to further research.

SCORING

Until the time of the AC21S project, little was known about scoring processes for collaborative problem solving. This was not surprising as very little was known about collaborative problem-solving itself. The ATC21S project therefore focused on existing frameworks for problem solving and collaborative learning and adapted these to collaborative problems. It was common to use a dichotomous success-failure scoring system which recorded whether the problem was solved and in doing so ignored the cognitive procedures involved.

This type of system was favoured because it was simple to use where specific problem-solving skills were being assessed. Greiff and Funke (2009) identified three measures which represented dynamic problem solving (DPS). These were Model Building, Forecasting and Information Retrieval. Students were awarded a false (0) or true (1) score to indicate they had solved the task. In contrast, the ATC21S project did not focus on success or failure on a task but decided to focus on how students collaboratively solved problems. The focus was on the process and quality of their collaboration and problem solving (PS) competence. There were clear differences between simple, dichotomously scored problem-solving tasks, dynamic problem solving, which used a series of dichotomous scores, and complex problem-solving tasks which used rubrics and partial credit scoring procedures.

Concerns about the procedural aspects of problem solving (PS) are not new (Polya, 1945, 1957; Schoenfeld, 1985). While aware of concerns, the ATC21S project through the Hesse (2012) framework outlined five broad components that were argued to represent collaborative problem-solving (CPS): participation, perspective taking, social regulation; and cognitive skills, task regulation and knowledge building. Within these five components, CPS defined 19 specific element or sub skills.

A set of assessment tasks, each tapping into a range of sub skills was developed. The tasks were meant to provide teachers with sufficient information to interpret students' capacity in the subskills, so that a profile of each student's performance could be developed for formative assessment and instructional purposes. Because of this approach, a robust automated scoring system was developed which focused on the process students used in solving collaborative problems. All this was undertaken in a context of unknowns. Scoring cognitive and social skills associated with the sub elements had never been done. Aligning the problem solving component with the Polya model, as in PISA, was equally problematic. Problem solving at an individual level is a covert process. Solving problem with a collaborative framework is an overt process demanding communication. In many ways Rumsfeld (2002) characterised the uncertainty.

The unknown unknowns are vastly more in number than the known unknowns, or the known knowns. We are in the peculiarly difficult position where we neither know what we know nor what we don't know. But we do know we don't know. Amidst this uncertainty what can we do? (Donald Rumsfeld, News briefing, U.S. Department of Defence, February 12, 2002).

PROCESS DATA STREAM

Recording detailed interactions between the student and the problem task was not new. Zoanetti (2010) used Bayes Nets to record these interactions in an unobtrusive way. Bennett, Jenkins, Persky, and Weiss, (2003) captured solution-process data and recorded this as a means of linking cognitive skill level and students social skill. Others evaluated the process and efficiency with which problem solvers completed tasks (Pelligrino, Chudowsky, & Glaser, 2001; Williamson, Mislevy, & Bejar, 2006). In the ATC21S context, actions and chat, and the placement of these, were coded and scored as descriptive purposeful actions. The tasks were designed to capture detailed interactions between the problem solver dyads as well as between the student and the task. The captured data from this process were described as a 'session log file'. They contained free-form data referred to as 'process stream data'. The log files were stored as 'free-form' text files with delimited strings of text, using a MySQL database architecture for recording the interactions with the tasks.

The process stream data described distinct key-strokes and mouse events such as typing, clicking, dragging, cursor movements, hovering time, action sequences and so on. In the database, each discrete action was recorded with a corresponding timestamp, which referenced the time at which an event occurred. A consistent format with a sequential numbering of events was used to facilitate comparison of records and tracking progress of events over time. Timestamps enabled detailed analysis of action and inaction, thus ensuring transparency of data storage and data processing. These forms of time-stamped data were described as "log-file data" and "process data" (Zoanetti, 2010). ATC21S used the term 'process stream data'.

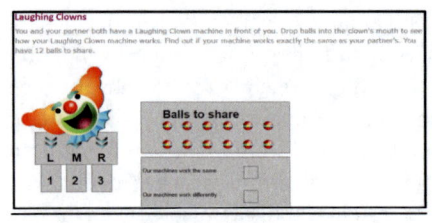

Student A View   Student B View

Figure 6.1. Student views

Each of 12 tasks enabled a variety of events to be categorised as common or unique events. 'Common' events applied to all collaborative assessment tasks. For example "Student (ID) has commenced task – task id" and the data captured would be "Records the start of a task.

Unique events within the process stream data were not common across assessment tasks. They applied to specific tasks due to the nature of the behaviours and interactions those tasks elicit. These data were defined using event types to match specific requirements that may arise only in a particular interactive problem space. Examples of such events for the Laughing Clowns task include "startDrag: ball_id; x, y coordinates of the ball at the start of the drag" and the data captured for that includes "Records the identifier of the ball and it's coordinates which is being dragged by the student" Both common and unique event types of process stream data were captured and recorded in a MySQL database and tagged with corresponding student identifier, task identifier, page identifier and role allocation of the acting student with time-stamping and appropriate indexing.

record	actor_pid	team_id	task_id	page	player_id	event	data	timestamp	Legends
127988	student0951	sng0076	103	1	A	start	Task started is 103	26/09/11 16:28	Checkbox
127989	student0952	sng0076	103	1	B	start	Task started is 103	26/09/11 16:28	startdrag
127995	student0951	sng0076	103	1	A	action	startDrag:ball1:410:35	26/09/11 16:29	stopdrag
127996	student0951	sng0076	103	1	A	action	stopDrag:ball1:188:129	26/09/11 16:29	dropshute
127997	student0951	sng0076	103	1	A	action	dropShuteR:ball1:188:129	26/09/11 16:29	chat
128001	student0952	sng0076	103	1	B	chat	You put where ?	26/09/11 16:29	start/end
128015	student0951	sng0076	103	1	A	chat	i put on r	26/09/11 16:29	
128017	student0951	sng0076	103	1	A	chat	landed on 1	26/09/11 16:29	
128019	student0952	sng0076	103	1	B	action	startDrag:ball7:410:85	26/09/11 16:29	
128021	student0951	sng0076	103	1	A	action	startDrag:ball10:485:85	26/09/11 16:29	
128034	student0952	sng0076	103	1	B	action	stopDrag:ball7:792:133	26/09/11 16:29	
128035	student0952	sng0076	103	1	B	action	dropShuteM:ball7:792:133	26/09/11 16:29	
128038	student0951	sng0076	103	1	A	action	startDrag:ball9:460:85	26/09/11 16:29	
128039	student0951	sng0076	103	1	A	action	stopDrag:ball9:102:132	26/09/11 16:29	
128041	student0951	sng0076	103	1	A	action	dropShuteL:ball9:102:132	26/09/11 16:29	
128048	student0951	sng0076	103	1	A	chat	all of it land on 1	26/09/11 16:29	
128049	student0952	sng0076	103	1	B	chat	I never see where it landed	26/09/11 16:29	
128053	student0952	sng0076	103	1	B	action	startDrag:ball8:435:85	26/09/11 16:29	
128056	student0952	sng0076	103	1	B	action	stopDrag:ball8:791:131	26/09/11 16:29	
128057	student0952	sng0076	103	1	B	action	dropShuteM:ball8:791:131	26/09/11 16:29	
128059	student0951	sng0076	103	1	A	action	startDrag:ball11:510:85	26/09/11 16:29	

Figure 6.2. A sample of log stream data

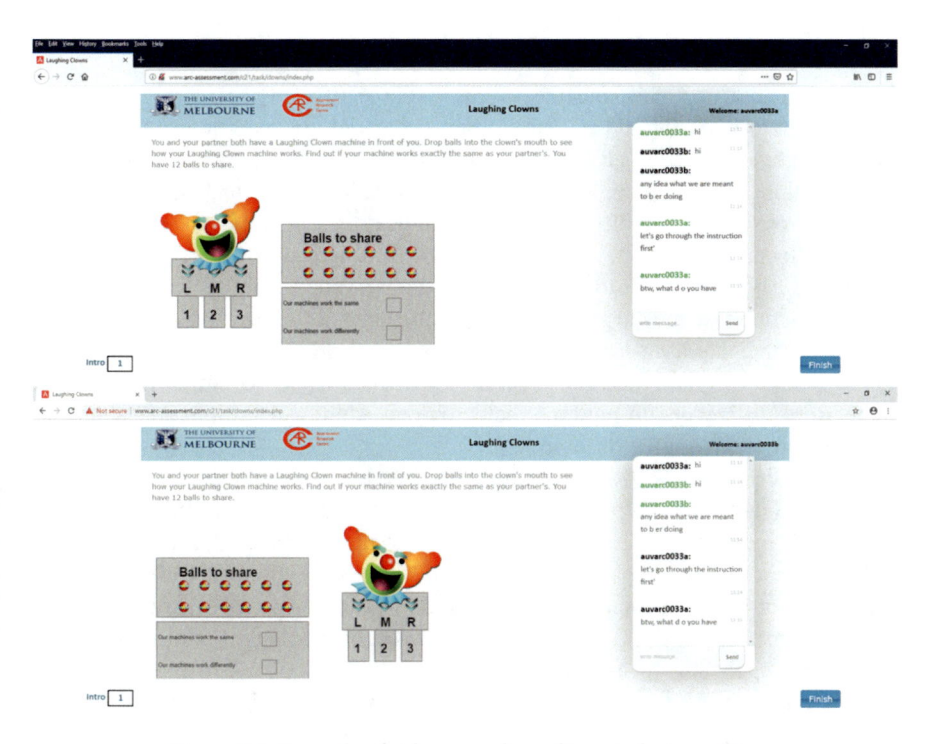

*Figure 6.3. Example of video recording of two students working
on the Laughing Clowns Task*

An excerpt of a session log for the Laughing Clowns Task can be seen in Figure 6.3. It represents the events that occurred while solving the problem by one team (two students). Both common and unique event types of process stream data were captured in string format and recorded in the MySQL database as a single row, tagged with corresponding student identifier, task identifier, page identifier and role allocation of the acting student in the collaborative session with time-stamping and appropriate indexing.

Each data set for each task was examined for behaviours and indicative patterns that could be interpreted as cognitive or social skills, linked to the 19 elements of the CPS framework defined by Hesse et al. (2012). These behaviours were then coded into rule-based algorithms that could extract them from the task process streams using a method pioneered by Zoanetti (2010). Zoanetti showed how process data (e.g., counts of actions) could be interpreted as an indicator of a behavioural variable (e.g., error avoidance or learning from mistakes). For example, in the Laughing Clowns task a count of the 'Drop Shute' actions (dropping the balls into the clown's mouth) can indicate how well the student managed their resources (the balls) and the frequency of the action occurring was interpreted as a pseudo measure of the action difficulty.

CODING

The coded indicators became the primary source of data for scoring and were classified into two main types – those that occur only in specific tasks and those that could be observed in all tasks were referred to as "global'. They included total response time, response time to partner questions, action counts, and other behaviours that were observed regardless of the task. Indicators that were task-specific were labelled 'local'. There were two categories of local indicators: direct and inferred. Direct indicators represent those that could be observed directly such as performing an action. Inferred indicators related to such things as sequences of action/chat. Patterns of indicators were used to infer the presence of indicative behaviours linked to the elements in the Hesse (2012) conceptual framework. Within these indicators there were differences in patterns that provided additional information about the relative complexity of the behaviour.

Each indicator was coded with a unique ID code. For example of the unique ID code 'U2L004A', 'U2' represents the Laughing Clowns task, 'L' indicates that it is a 'local' indicator specific to that task ('G' would represent that it was a global indicator that could be applied to all tasks), '004' is a numerical code specific to this indicator and is sequential within each task (in this case 004 it was the fourth indicator created for this task) provided for ease of referencing, 'A' indicates that this indicator is applicable to student A.

The indicators were then defined in the process stream using search algorithms. For example, counting the occurrences of the event 'chat' in the process stream provided the frequency of the chat and the frequency provided a pseudo measure of action difficulty, which, when linked to the Hesse framework element enabled the estimation of the relative difficulty of the element. The process was complex, but it worked. The issue was the complexity of the process and the idiosyncrasy of the data for each task. There were too few common or unique indicators and it meant that every task had to be calibrated separately and then linked together in a single construct using common person equating. Moreover, for each new task, a new set of indicators had to be defined and a new sample of students exposed to the tasks. The tasks were then or anchored to existing cps tasks. It became a laborious, inefficient, expensive and error prone process.

EXISTING CPS FRAMEWORKS

The PISA framework defines CPS as a personal attribute measured through a set of 12 skills. There is currently little detail published on the specifics of these skills and observable measures or levels of ability. The CPS skills proposed by OECD present as composites of multiple behaviours required for the actions, processes and strategies employed by students. The Hesse et al. (2015) framework developed as part of the ATC21S project focuses on the specific subskills, or elements, required of proficient collaborative problem solvers along with observable behaviours expected across a

Table 6.1. Process comparison

CPS process Framework (This study)	ATC21S (Griffin & Care, 2012)	PISA CPS (OECD, 2013)	CRESST CPS (O'Neil, 1999)	Polya PS (1945)	Sternberg PS (1997)	Garofalo & Lester PS (1985)	Greiff & Funke Complex PS (2009)
Exploring		Exploring and understanding			Identify the problem	Orientation	Information retrieval
Defining	Problem analysis: information collection and linking	Representing and formulating; Establishing and maintaining	Content understanding	Understand the problem	Define the problem		Model building
Planning	Goal setting	Planning and executing; Taking appropriate action to solve the problem		Devise a plan	Organize the information; Allocate resources	Organization	Forecasting
Strategising	Resouce management; Systematicity		Problem solving strategies	Carry out the plan	Select a strategy	Execution	Reduction of information
Evaluating	Identifying cause and effect	Monitoring and reflecting; Establishing and maintaining team organization		Look back and check	Moniter the solution; Evaluate success	Verification	Priority setting and evaluation
Reflecting	Reflect and monitors: Tests alternative hypothesises		Self-regulation				

continuum of ability but it does not present a framework from a process perspective. The ATC21S project did however outline the need to address the tension between skills and processes as a necessary point of future research (Hesse et al., 2015).

The procedural aspects of problem solving, in particular, have been considered important for some years (Polya, 1945, 1957; Schoenfeld, 1985). Numerous phase models of problem solving have been described in the literature with two distinct perspectives: descriptive phase models and prescriptive phase models. While descriptive models outline that people go through various linear phases in the process of solving problems, prescriptive models suggest what those phases are and that people are more successful if a particular order of phases is followed. Much of the argument for these phase models is rooted in logic and observations have not yet been made directly from behaviours of problem solvers. In contrast, there are fewer frameworks that outline the process of collaboration. Table 6.4 presents the process in this study which highlights CPS as a complex skill. Also presented are the processes outlined in the PISA CPS and CRESST CPS frameworks which, while outlining CPS, combine separate frameworks of problem solving and collaboration in to one single framework. Further, key frameworks of problem solving are presented for comparison. The processes from other frameworks are mapped to the process outlined in this study, not to suggest equivalence but to suggest an alignment in the language and content of the processes.

A GROUNDED FRAMEWORK

Work continued the repackaging of the tasks from the ATC21S project implementing CPS assessment research. With every application, observers became aware of systematic behaviour patterns of dyads when working through CPS tasks. Once this was realised, a formal, systematic approached was developed for observing and interpreting student behaviour patterns exhibited by collaborative problem solvers. It also became clear that the behaviour patterns were not necessarily dependent on the task or the nature of the students solving the problem. Slowly, the observers revealed the essence of the common process and hypothesised an alternate framework to those proposed by Hesse et al and PISA. The major point of departure was the realisations that

1. The frequency of activity occurrence provided a pseudo measure of difficulty.
2. People followed roughly similar process of
   a. exploring the problem space
   b. defining the problem and its sources
   c. planning an approach
   d. refining the process to identify strategies
   e. evaluating the effect of the strategy
   f. reflecting on its solution and checking for better solutions.
3. They also identified a series of behaviours that were consistent with collaboration, but not with group or team work. Each dyad exhibited the same pattern of skills in that they
   a. shared common goal or focus

   b. each contributed unique resource to the problem resolution where the resources they contributed were not possessed by the partner, observed that the problem could not be resolved unless all contributed;

   c. realised that they benefited from the contribution of the partners and the partners benefited from their contribution;

   d. learned to trust and depend on the partner contributing in areas they could not and it was clear that the partner had learned to trust and depend on them.

4. These four behaviour categories defined the boundary or criteria of collaboration and enabled a separation of the collaboration process from group work and team work. Unless all four were present the collaborative problem-solving task could not be resolved. Moreover, there was a hierarchy of difficulty associated with the four categories of behaviours. Log stream data were used to search for evidence of the four categories and it became evident that the hierarchy followed the sequence – focus, contribute benefit and depend. The behavioural categories are defined as capabilities as each can be taught and learned.

These grounded observations were then used to form a new conceptual framework.

PROPOSED FRAMEWORK

The logic of the CPS Process framework presented here is that proficient collaborative problem solvers begin by exploring both the social space and then the problem space. They define the problem from careful examination of their joint resources, developing a shared understanding of the problem. Students then develop a plan and strategize, applying the plan. Students evaluated their progress before reflecting and monitoring their outcomes, considering alternative hypotheses. The process is anticipated to be iterative in that students are likely to regress to a previous process depending upon the complexity of the task. Each capability is presented at the earliest point in which it needs to be demonstrated.

Exploring

The first capability, explore, relies on students searching the social space and exploring the problem space. Students' first reactions would likely be to engage with and explore the task space to build an understanding of the problem. Their actions with both the task and their role could guide their understanding of the importance of their own contributions to task success. Ability to interact with others and recognise the importance of that interaction would also contribute to their success.

Defining

The second capability focusing on students jointly defining the problem. Problems are not typically well defined and the tasks developed in this project were ill defined as a direct reflection of this. In the classroom, students are typically presented with well-defined problems and are likely not be familiar with this type of problem space, therefore, building a shared understanding of the problem is considered essential for collaboration (Barron, 2003). Students' understanding and awareness of others is likely to evolve as the collaborative relationship progresses and students adapt their communication and clarify the problem for others. Students needed to collect information from both the task space and from partners and even identify gaps in their understanding. They needed to manage resources, exchanging information and integrating resources to build their mutual understanding of the problem and what was required to solve it.

The definition of this capability is informed in part by existing problem solving literature. Polya's problem solving process of 'understanding the problem' suggests students need to be familiarised with the problem. This process also draws on PISA's problem solving process 'exploring and understanding' involving the interpretation of information presented and subsequently discovered through exploration in order to understand the problem space. They suggest that successful problem solvers would need to interpret the information that is provided to them as well as explore for further information (OECD, 2012).

In a CPS context these processes would include students familiarising themselves and others with the problem and actively engaging and communicating with others and act in order to come to a common understanding. PISA's CPS framework identifies a collaborative component of 'establishing and maintaining shared understanding' in which they determine that students should establish mutual understanding of the problem by identifying what each other knows about the problem. They identify the importance of students identifying the perspective of others in establishing a shared vision of the problem and activities (OECD, 2013). The PISA framework recognises that in defining the problem in CPS, the nature of communication is important and activities such as verifying what each knows and sharing that information are necessary skills for building a shared understanding.

The Hesse et al. (2014) framework highlights the importance of defining the problem in two of their social strands: participation and perspective taking. The participation strand assesses the extent to which students engage with the problem space as well as the extent that they communicate with others (Hesse et al., 2014). Defining a problem collaboratively is enhanced by students' ability to take the perspective of others. Perspective taking is related to students' ability to understand the spatial or psychological perspective of others. Students who are lacking in this may assume other's perspectives are aligned with theirs. Perspective taking is especially relevant as recognising there are differing perspectives and understanding those perspectives have a positive effect on students' ability to engage in their role and with others, and communicate. Initial steps in perspective taking were likely have positive implications for future capabilities in the process.

Planning

Once students have a shared understanding of the problem they can begin to plan a course of action. Planning is the process of thinking of a predetermined course of action or set of steps required to achieve a goal or target. Planning refers to students' ability to develop strategies based on the steps required to solve the problem. In the context of CPS, plans needed to address a shared problem and provide the basis for a coordinated problem solution (Weldon & Weingart, 1993). The ability to plan is an important skill in solving problems both independently and collaboratively. The project tasks assessed students' collaboration through computer-supported chat messages or during essay writing tasks. It emerged that discussing plans regarding how to approach the task and negotiating joint efforts improved the quality of their collaborative outcomes.

When solving problems collaboratively, planning refers to the formulation of hypotheses and selection of steps to achieve the goal (Hesse et al., 2015). Joint planning is more complex than planning independently. The overt/covert distinction in CPS needs to be understood by the problem solvers. They need to draw on their mutually derived understanding to jointly analyse and hypothesise solutions to the problem from which they can set joint goals. Planning during collaborative problem solving can be challenging especially if one or more students are finding it difficult to understand the problem or they haven't been particularly successful in the first instance and maintain different understandings of the problem.

Students who persevere in planning ahead are those who acknowledge the benefits of doing so. For example, if students notice improved performance in their strategy such as decreases in time, number of moves or amount of errors then they are more likely to increase their amount of planning. Sacerdoti (1975) suggested that the plans follow an orderly path as the plan expands into sub-plans before culminating in the goal state. Others suggest that planning is not always as systematic but can be opportunistic, based on the circumstance, and can evolve during the process. They highlighted that previous planning expertise can impact on a student's ability to adopt useful planning methods. Students who are familiar with the problem space may adopt frequently used or well-refined methods for planning or they may be able to apply opportunistic methods in a timely manner due to experience.

Strategising

The process of strategising in CPS refers to the way in which students approach CPS tasks and their implementation of plans and strategies to solve the problem. Students jointly apply their knowledge in the task space and test their hypotheses to achieve their common goal. Students who are proficient take a systematic approach to reaching the solution, executing plans from the joint planning process. There is little previous literature that directly investigates the process of students' joint approach to attempting to solve the problem. PISA's CPS framework attempts to address this process through their collaborative component 'taking appropriate action to solve the problem'. This component refers to the joint effort of students to take action in a task and follow the appropriate steps to solve the problem (OECD, 2013).

Existing PS frameworks contribute theory towards this process such as Polya's (1957) third problem solving process, carrying out a plan, and PISA's (2012) PS process of 'executing'. They suggest that problem solvers need to implement their action steps, putting their plan into action. Additionally, in a CPS context, the students need to implement the plan jointly while recognising the contributions of others. Zagal et al. (2006) suggested that there should be a 'tension' between the individual and the group in that the best actions for the individual are not perhaps the best actions for the group. Students are encouraged to adopt a collaborative approach when they experience difficulties working individually. In facilitating these social dilemmas Axelrod (1984) noted that increasing frequencies of interaction and reporting information about own actions were useful strategies. Individual participation and contributions are not necessarily considered antecedent conditions, but they can be perceived as pre-requisite characteristics of effective group work (Mickan & Rodger, 2000).

Evaluating

Evaluating shared progress of the problem throughout the task is, by definition, critical to collaboration (Roschelle & Teasley, 1994). Problem solvers need to periodically evaluate progress throughout the CPS journey to identify what is working and what is not. Evaluating progress helps collaborators to make any necessary adjustments but also informs future activities. To effectively replicate best practices in solving problems, evolving understanding should be shared with the group. In Dillenbourg and Traum's (2006) theory of 'grounding', misunderstandings become learning opportunities for students. Students are required to evaluate the efforts of their collaborators and attempt to repair misunderstandings by explaining, justifying and making knowledge explicit. It is important that students evaluate their shared progress and understanding of the problem in order to recognise any variations as they arise and rectify misunderstandings before they impede joint work (Roschelle & Teasley, 1994).

Reflecting

Polya's (1957) process requires that students need to be reflective and review the entire process. He suggests that this may allow alternative methods to become clear. Similarly, PISA's final problem-solving process is 'evaluating and reflecting' involves reflecting on the plan to evaluate whether another approach would be more suitable, whether initial solutions were appropriate and whether assumptions hold. This is by revisiting initial hypotheses (OECD, 2012). In a CPS context, these problem-solving processes can still be applicable but extend the focus of the reflections to involve other players. In a CPS context, students must continually reflect on and check their own and others understanding to ensure they are aligned. If adaptions or modifications need to be made students may return to the joint planning stage to reorganise information, alter hypotheses and plans or set alternative goals. Collaborative components from the PISA CPS framework specify the importance of maintaining shared understanding and group organisation throughout the task. These collaborative components focus on monitoring results, evaluating the success of the plan and repairing misunderstandings to ensure optimum collaborative problem solving (OECD, 2013).

VALIDATING THE FRAMEWORK

The Collaborative Problem Solving (CPS) Process Framework defines CPS as a unified construct. Other contributions to the field present CPS as an amalgamation of collaboration and problem-solving frameworks. There is no framework in the current literature which presents the CPS processes based on the identification of CPS as a competence rather than a cohesive set of and complex skills.

The grounded framework presents the CPS process as consisting of six capabilities: in the few years since the ATC 21S project was completed there has been considerable uptake of the materials and a burgeoning interest in collaborative problem-solving. The two major players in this process, PISA and ATC21S attempted to develop new and engaging tasks. However they have been beset by difficulties of scoring and interpreting student performances. PISA found a partial solution by having one of the agents as a character in a computer play. This enabled tight control on one aspect of the collaboration in problem-solving task.

ATC21S maintained the position that collaboration had to be between two persons. This paper focuses on the work of ATC 21S because of the problems experienced when developing new items. Because the coding system developed during the ATC 21 project was idiosyncratic to the task every new item developed had to be trialled with large numbers of students in order to generate sufficient data to apply the principles of coding and scoring as outlined in the volume edited by Griffin and Care (2014). This meant that the cost of developing new items was prohibitive and a more generic method of coding people's behaviour in collaboratively solving problems had to be found.

Through a mixture of direct observation, think aloud protocols and interviews a set of capabilities were identified that successful collaborative problem solvers needed to develop. In addressing the problem the collaborating group needs to jointly explore the problem space, define the nature of the problem, plan an approach, strategise the process of resolving the issue, evaluate the solution and the process, and reflect on the quality of the strategy and solution. Each of these must be undertaken in a collaborative fashion. Again by direct observation of students solving collaborative problems it has been possible to identify five indicators of collaboration for each of the six capabilities (exploring, defining, planning, strategizing, evaluating and reflecting).

Table 6.2. CPS process framework

				Criteria			
Indicators	D. Depend	Asks others about their resources and ideas	Asks for feedback/ contribution from others	Discusses relevant resources before commencing trialling	Takes turns to identify outcomes of trialling	Negotiates to successfully resolve conflict with others	Discusses alternative approaches
	C. Benefit	Supplements own resources with examples from others	Asks others about their resources	Allocate roles within the plan	Integrates other contributions into own actions	Negotiates in an attempt to resolve conflict with others	Asks others for feedback on task outcome
	B. Contribute	Describes resources to a partner	Responds to others questions	Discuss joint plan with sequential steps	Directs others to use resources	Shares conflict with others	Tells others task outcome
	A. Focus (Independent)	Makes a list of resources under their own control	Describes own resources to others	Suggests general plan to others	Reports outcomes of actions to others	Completes task	Reviews task before completing
		1. Exploring	2. Defining	3. Planning	4. Strategising	5. Evaluating	6. Reflecting
				Capabilities			

Collaboration occurred for each of these capabilities but the problem solvers shared a single focus, when they were each able to contribute to the process; there was clear benefit to each person from the actions of the other; an acceptance of the necessity that they depend upon a collaborative partners; and an acceptance that they could improve their own collaboration efforts through metacognition. These indicators of collaboration were observed within each of the capabilities in a hierarchical fashion. Shared focus was considered to be the easiest of the indicators in that any progress to be made in any of the six capabilities the players must at first share a common goal. It was also observed more often than any other indicated as players attempted to identify the nature of the problem.

Metacognitive exercises represented the most difficult and few of the observed subjects reported this analysis of their own thinking and contribution to collaboration. Only students with the highest level of proficiency in each of the six capabilities demonstrate this level of sophistication in reviewing their contribution to collaboration. For example, a player may present as 'depending' during exploration, but only 'contributing' while 'reflecting'. The most proficient collaborative problem solvers demonstrate 'metacognitive' levels across each of the capabilities. In Table 6.1 each of the cells contains an example criterion. The criteria are versions of the indicative behaviours rephrased to describe a level of quality for each of these indicative behaviours.

For example, a common focus in exploration would be characterised by "making a list of resources under their control", contributing during exploration would be characterised by "describing resources to a partner"; benefiting from others during exploration would be characterised by "supplementing own resources with examples from others"; accepting dependence in the exploration phase would be characterised by "asking others about their resources and ideas"; being metacognitive during exploration phase could be characterised by examining "the process of contributing benefiting resources". Each of these examples in the framework treats the indicator of collaboration as a dichotomy. Rephrasing the criteria in each of the cells of the chart would enable a partial credit model to be developed.

Table 6.2 presents the proposed CPS Process Framework. The validation steps, presented in the next section, presents a plan for identifying supporting evidence for the framework and establishing an empirical developmental progression.

VALIDATION

1. *Observations.* Each of the observers documented the activities of a cohort of students completing the tasks and coded their behaviour using the criteria in the proposed CPS framework (taking notes on the actions observed for each box in the grid). The observed behaviours are described in a series of rubrics, and examples of these are presented in Table 6.4. These data were reorganised into a Guttman chart (Griffin, Francis, & Robertson, 2017). Time stamped coded observations were cross checked with the log files to identify indicative log data at the same time-stamped event. In this way observed behaviours were matched to log file traces which in turn could be used to construct search algorithms. The algorithms were then used to identify similar behaviours in other data files.

2. *Scoring.* The criteria in each of the cells in Table 6.1 were used such that student behaviours could be coded as present or absent. This procedure was used to derive dichotomous scoring rule for each criterion which was then applied for each criterion for each student. Search algorithms were then used to identify time stamped and matched strings in the log files for each criterion nested within students across all tasks.

3. *Analysis.* The search algorithms were used to examine the data in the log files for approximately 2000 students. The coded data was presented in an ASCII file suitable for analysis. The first step was to calibrate the criteria using IRT, and from that preliminary analysis it was possible to make adjustments to the criteria and coding procedures where necessary.

Observations

Ten pairs (20 students) were video and audio recorded completing one bundle of ATC21S CPS tasks (Laughing Clowns, Plant Growth, and Balance Beam). An example of the video arrangement is presented in Figure 6.1. Student A can be viewed in the top left quadrant, and their screen perspective in the top right quadrant. Student B can be observed in the bottom left quadrant, with their screen perspective in the bottom right quadrant. In addition to typing their communication (chats) to one another in the chat box, they were asked to think aloud to communicate their thought processes as they worked through the task.

Students were observed and their behaviour coded according to each criterion. Student chats, actions and think aloud behaviour were used as indicative of the presence or absence of each criterion behaviour. For example, where a student was observed describing their own resources to others (Defining/Contribute), the code of 1 was recorded for the criterion 1 in that cell of the framework if the behaviour was observed as present, or a 0 if this behaviour was not demonstrated. In addition, video and audio recording data was triangulated with the log file data. Sections of log files were highlighted from each team that were perceived to be relevant to each of the capabilities in the process.

This log file analysis demonstrated evidence of the criteria in the framework. Differences between observers and between methods were resolved and codes aggregated into one chart presented in Table 6.2. Each row presents a student, and each column represents a criterion. For example, 1A represents the capability Exploring (1) and the indicator Focus (A). ("Makes a list of resources. Under their own control"). Totals for each student and item are computed. In Table 6.2, students are listed vertical left-hand column on criterion across the table.

The data were arranged as a Guttman chart to enable a visual representation of the coding. The chart orders student performance according to student demonstrated proficiency, and orders assessment items according to their difficulty.

The Guttman chart allows a qualitative review of the framework and its capacity to be used as a scoring mechanism for CPS assessments. The extent to which the data aligns with the theoretical interpretation of the constructs can analysed.

SCORE GENERATION

The construct was defined and a metric defining a person's level on that construct was derived through a behavioural analysis of process data. Process data was generated by capturing all actions and chat communications completed by the student during task play and stored in time series log files. Scoring behaviours have been developed for each of the criteria in the theoretical CPS Process Framework. The theoretical framework is intended to represent the construct regardless of environment or number of collaborators. The scoring framework is specified to the ATC21S online task environment. However, the behaviours are designed to be generalisable across all ATC21S tasks and student roles. These scoring behaviours are presented in the appropriate grid box in Table 6.3, relevant to the criterion they are identified to be indicative of. For example, criterion '1B Exploring/Contributing' is giving their own resources to others. This can be interpreted in the specific task space as 'passing their resources to their partner'.

Table 6.3. Guttman analysis of the scored outcomes

Criteria	Code	085b	086a	085a	055b	088b	054a	058b	090b	056a	090a	059a	087b	088a	055a	054b	058a	056b	059b	086b	087a	Total
		27	27	26	25	25	24	24	22	21	21	21	20	19	18	14	11	10	9	6	6	
Follows sequential action steps of plan	4E	0	0	0	0	0	0	0	0	0	0	0	0	0	0	0	0	0	0	0	0	0
Develops shared action plan with sequential steps	3E	0	0	0	0	0	0	0	0	0	0	0	0	0	0	0	0	0	0	0	0	0
Implements alternative approaches	6E	0	0	1	0	0	0	0	0	0	0	0	0	1	0	0	0	0	0	1	0	4
Discusses alternative approaches together	6D	1	1	1	0	0	0	0	0	0	0	0	0	0	0	0	0	0	0	0	1	4
Agrees on task outcomes	5E	1	1	1	1	0	0	0	0	0	0	0	0	0	0	0	0	0	0	0	1	5
Reviews tasks before completing	6A	1	1	1	1	0	0	0	0	0	0	0	0	0	0	0	0	0	0	0	1	5
Asks others for feedback on task outcome	6C	1	0	1	0	1	1	0	1	0	0	0	0	0	0	0	0	0	0	0	0	6
Negotiates to successfully resolve conflict with others	5D	1	1	1	0	1	1	1	1	0	1	1	0	0	0	0	0	0	0	0	0	9
Discuss joint plan with sequential steps	3C	1	1	0	1	1	1	1	1	1	0	1	0	0	0	0	0	0	0	0	0	9
Tells others task outcome	6B	1	1	1	1	1	1	1	0	1	0	0	1	0	0	0	0	0	0	0	0	11
Takes turns to identify outcomes of trialing	4D	1	1	0	1	1	1	1	0	1	0	1	1	0	0	1	1	0	0	0	0	12
Asks for feedback/contribution from others	2D	1	1	1	1	1	1	1	1	1	1	1	0	0	0	0	0	0	0	0	0	12
Negotiates in an attempt to resolve conflict with others	5C	1	1	1	1	1	1	1	1	1	1	1	1	0	0	0	0	0	0	0	0	13
Discusses relevant resources before commencing trialing	3D	1	1	0	1	1	1	1	0	1	1	1	1	0	1	0	0	1	0	0	0	14
Responds to other's questions	2C	1	1	1	1	1	1	1	1	1	1	1	1	0	0	0	0	0	0	0	0	14
Examines shared resources	1E	1	1	1	1	1	1	1	1	1	1	1	1	1	0	0	0	0	0	0	0	15
Shares conflict with others	5B	1	1	1	1	1	0	1	1	1	1	1	1	0	0	1	0	0	0	0	0	15
Describes own resources to others	2B	1	1	1	1	1	1	1	1	0	1	1	0	1	1	0	0	0	0	1	0	15
Reports outcomes of actions to others	4A	1	1	1	1	1	1	1	1	1	1	1	1	0	0	0	0	1	0	0	0	15
Agrees on definition of problem	2E	1	1	1	1	1	1	1	1	1	1	0	1	1	0	0	0	0	0	0	0	16
Asks/enquires other other's resources	1D	1	1	1	1	1	1	1	1	1	1	1	1	0	0	1	0	0	0	0	0	16
Take and uses others resources	1C	1	1	1	1	1	1	1	1	1	1	1	1	0	0	0	0	0	0	0	0	16
Describes own resources to others	3B	1	1	1	1	1	1	1	1	1	1	1	1	0	0	0	0	0	0	0	0	16
Integrates other contributions to own actions	4C	1	1	1	1	1	1	1	1	1	1	1	1	0	1	0	1	0	0	0	0	17
Directs others to use resources	4B	1	1	1	1	1	1	1	1	1	1	1	1	0	1	0	0	0	0	0	0	17
Gives own resources/information to others	1B	1	1	1	1	1	1	1	1	1	1	1	1	1	1	1	1	1	1	1	1	20
Completes task	5A	1	1	1	1	1	1	1	1	1	1	1	1	1	1	1	1	1	1	1	1	20
Develops general pan	3A	1	1	1	1	1	1	1	1	1	1	1	1	1	1	1	1	1	1	1	1	20
Uses only own resources	2A	1	1	1	1	1	1	1	1	1	1	1	1	1	1	1	1	1	1	1	1	20
Manipulate own resources	1A	1	1	1	1	1	1	1	1	1	1	1	1	1	1	1	1	1	1	1	1	20

Search algorithms were generated to seek each of these scoring behaviours in the process data. If the behaviour is present it is recorded as '1', if absent then '0'. If the behaviour is not applicable, such as the student did not reach that point of the task, the behaviour was recorded as '-1', missing. Each of the scoring behaviours is sought for each student in each task. It was also important to code the outcome (correct/incorrect solution) and use this for validation purposes.

Collaboration Instrument Sample Items

KSAVE and discovery – collaboration knowledge

☐ **Q7** **When I interact effectively with others, they are most likely to do which of the following? They are likely to …**

> Know when it is appropriate to listen and when to speak
> Speak with clarity and awareness of audience and purpose
> Listen with care, patience and honesty
> Behave in a respectful manner
> understand turn taking in conversations

☐ **Q8** **When I work in diverse teams, I need to do ONE of the following …**

> recognize the individual roles in a successful team
> know my own strengths and weaknesses
> accept the strengths and weaknesses in others

☐ **Q9** **When working in teams, I need to leverage social and cultural differences to emphasize which ONE of the following?**

> create new ideas
> increase innovation and implementation
> maintain the quality of my performance

☐ **Q11** **When maintaining projects WE need to plan, set and ACHIEVE shared goals, and then which ONE is the most important.**

> monitor and re-plan in the light of unforeseen developments
> Prioritize and plan to achieve the intended group result
> Persevere to achieve goals
> overcome obstacles ad competing ideas

☐ **Q12** **I can help others towards the achievement of a shared goal by using any of the following strategies. Rank each strategy in order of effectiveness for you.**

	1lo	2	3	4	5hi	0n/a

> Use interpersonal skills to influence towards a goal
> Use problem solving skills to guide others toward a goal
> Leverage strengths of others to accomplish a common goal
> Inspire others to reach their best via example

Table 6.4. Scoring interpretation of the CPS process framework

Indicators		Criteria					
	D. Depend	1. Presence of questions (keyword) in chat 2. Count of questions in chat		Presence of only relevant resources keywords in chat	1. Presence of move resource from student, followed by partner, then repeat once	1. Different answers, followed by chat, followed by change to same answer 2. Both finish task together	
	C. Benefit	1. Presence of others resources accepted and moved	Presence of question keyword and resource keyword in same chat line		1. Presence of question and partner resource from student in same chat line 2. Presence of resource keyword in partner chat, followed by student manipulating that resource	1. Different answers, followed by chat	1. Presence of resource keyword before entering own solution
	B. Contribute	1. Passes resource to others 2. Presence of chat 3. Count of chat lines	Partner asks question followed by student responding chat		1. Presence of partners resource in chat before partner manipulates that resource		1. Tells partner their own solution after they have entered it
	A. Focus (Independent)	1. Presence of own resource moved 2. Count number of own resources moved	Chat containing own resource keywords	Chats to partner before entering rule	1. Presence of resource keyword in chat after manipulation of that resource	1. Finishes task	1. Selects review before finishing
		1. Exploring	*2. Defining*	*3. Planning*	*4. Strategising*	*5. Evaluating*	*6. Reflecting*
		Capabilities					

REFERENCES

Barron, B. (2000). Achieving coordination in collaborative problem-solving groups. *The Journal of the Learning Sciences, 9*(4), 403–436.

Bennett, R. E., Persky, H., Weiss, A., & Jenkins, F. (2007). *Problem solving in technology-rich environments: A report from the NAEP technology-based assessment project* (NCES 2007–466).

Washington, DC: National Center for Education Statistics. Retrieved from http://nces.ed.gov/pubsearch/pubsinfo.asp?pubid=2007466

Care, E., Griffin, P., Scoular, C., Awwal, N., & Zoanetti, N. (2015). Collaborative problem solving tasks. In P. Griffin & E. Care (Eds.), *Assessment and teaching of 21st century skills: Methods and approach* (pp. 85–104). Dordrecht: Springer.

Care, E., Griffin, P., & Wilson, M. (2017). *Research in collaborativev problem solving; Assessment and teaching 21st century skills.* Dordrecht: Springer.

Care, E., Scoular, C., & Griffin, P. (2016). Assessment of collaborative problem solving in education environments. *Applied Measurement in Education, 29*(4), 250–264.

Clark, H. H. (1996). *Using language.* Cambridge: Cambridge University Press.

Clark, H. H., & Brennan, S. E. (1991). Grounding in communication. In L. B. Resnick, J. M. Levine, & S. D. Teasley (Eds.), *Perspectives on socially shared cognition* (pp. 127–149). Washington, DC: American Psychological Association.

Dillenbourg, P. (1999). What do you mean by 'collaborative learning'? In P. Dillenbourg (Ed.), *Collaborative-learning: Cognitive and computational approaches* (pp. 1–19). Oxford: Elsevier.

Dillenbourg, P., Baker, M., Blaye, A., & O'Malley, C. (1996). The evolution of research on collaborative learning. In E. Spada & P. Reiman (Eds.), *Learning in humans and machine: Towards an interdisciplinary learning science* (pp. 189–211). Oxford: Elsevier.

Dillenbourg, P., & Traum, D. (2006). Sharing solutions: Persistence and grounding in multi-modal collaborative problem solving. *The Journal of the Learning Sciences, 15*, 121–151.

Gillis, S., & Griffin, P. (2005). Principles underpinning graded assessment in VET: A critique of prevailing perceptions. *International Journal of Training Research, 3*(1), 53–81.

Graesser, A. C., & McDaniel, B. (2008). Conversational agents can provide formative assessment, constructive learning, and adaptive instruction. In C. Dwyer (Ed.), *The future of assessment: Shaping teaching and learning* (pp. 85–112). Mahwah, NJ: Lawrence Erlbaum Associates.

Grieff, S., & Funke, J. (2009). Measuring complex problem solving: The MicroDYN approach. In F. Scheuermann & J. Bjornsson (Eds.), *The transition to computer-based assessment: Lessons learned from large –scale surveys and implications for testing* (pp. 157–163). Luxembourg: Office for Official Publications of the European Communicates.

Griffin, P., & Care, E. (Eds.). (2015). *Assessment and teaching 21st century skills: Methods and approach.* Dordrecht: Springer.

Griffin, P., & Francis, M. (2014). Developing rubrics. In P. Griffin (Ed.), *Assessment for teaching.* Melbourne: Cambridge University Press.

Griffin, P., Francis, M., & Robertson, P. (2017). Judgment Based assessment. In P. Griffin (Ed.), *Assessment for teaching.* Melbourne: Cambridge University Press.

Griffin, P., Gillis, S., & Calvitto, L. (2007). Standards-referenced assessment for Vocational education and training in schools. *Australian Journal of Education, 51*(1), 19–38.

Griffin, P., McGaw, B., & Care, E. (Eds.). (2012). *Assessment and teaching 21st century skills.* Dordrecht: Springer.

Guttman, L. A. (1944). A basis for scaling qualitative data. *American Sociological Review, 91*, 139–150.

Hesse, F., Care, E., Buder, J., Sassenberg, K., & Griffin, P. (2014). A framework for teachable collaborative problem solving skills. In P. Griffin & E. Care (Eds.), *Assessment and teaching of 21st century skills: Methods and approach.* Dordrecht: Springer.

Mickan, S., & Rodger, S. (2000). Characteristics of effective teams: A literature review. *Australian Health Review, 23*(3), 201–208.

O'Neil, H. F. (1999). Perspectives on computer-based performance assessment of problem solving: Editor's introduction. *Computers in Human Behavior, 15*, 255–268.

O'Neil, H. F., Chung, G., & Brown, R. (1997). Use of networked simulations as a context to measure team competencies. In H. F. O'Neil (Ed.), *Workforce readiness: Competencies and assessment* (pp. 411–452). Mahwah, NJ: Lawrence Erlbaum Associates.

O'Neil, H. F., Chuang, S., & Chung, G. K. W. K. (2004). Issues in the computer-based assessment of collaborative problem solving. *Assessment in Education, 10*, 361–373.

Organisation for Economic Co-operation and Development (OECD). (2013). *PISA 2015: Draft collaborative problem solving framework*. Retrieved from http://www.oecd.org/callsfortenders/ Annex%20ID_PISA%202015%20Collaborative%20Problem%20Solving%20Framework%20.pdf

Pellegrino, J. W., Chudowsky, N., & Glaser, R. (2001). *Knowing what students know: The science and design of educational assessment*. Washington, DC: National Research Council, National Academy Press.

Polya, G. (1945). *How to solve it: A new aspect of mathematical method*. Princeton, NJ: Princeton University Press.

Rasch, G. (1960). *Probabilistic models for some intelligence and attainment tests*. Chicago, IL: The University of Chicago Press.

Roschelle, J. (1992). Learning by collaborating: Convergent conceptual change. *The Journal of the Learning Sciences, 2*(3), 235–276.

Schoenfeld, A. H. (1985). *Mathematical problem solving*. New York, NY: Academic Press.

Schoenfeld, A. H. (1999). Looking toward the 21st century: Challenges of educational theory and practice. *Educational Researcher, 28*, 4–14.

Schoenfeld, A. H. (2013). Reflections on problem solving theory and practice. *The Mathematics Enthusiast, 10*(1), 9–34.

Stevens, M. J., & Campion, M. A. (1994). The knowledge, skills and ability requirements for teamwork: Implications for human resources management. *Journal of Management, 20*(2), 502–528.

Vygotsky, L. S. (1978). *Interactions between learning and development. Mind and society: The development of higher mental processes*. Cambridge, MA: Harvard University Press.

Vygotsky, L. S. (1986). *Thought and language*. Cambridge, MA: The MIT Press.

Weldon, E., & Weingart, L. R. (1993). Group goals and group performance. *British Journal of Social Psychology, 32*(4), 307–334.

Williamson, D. M., Mislevy, R. J., & Bejar, I. I. (2006). *Automated scoring of complex tasks in computer-based testing*. Mahwah, NJ: Lawrence Erlbaum Associates.

Zagal, J. P., Rick, J., & His, I. (2006). Collaborative games: Lessons learned from board games. *Simulation and Gaming, 37*(1), 24–40.

Zoanetti, N. (2010). Interactive computer based assessment tasks: How problem-solving process data can inform instruction. *Australasian Journal of Educational Technology, 26*(5), 585–606.

Patrick Griffin
Melbourne Graduate School of Education
The University of Melbourne
Australia

Nafisa Awwal
Melbourne Graduate School of Education
The University of Melbourne
Australia

BAHAR HASIRCI, DIDEM KARAKUZULAR
AND DERIN ATAY

7. ASSESSMENT LITERACY OF TURKISH TEACHERS OF ENGLISH LANGUAGE

A Comparative Study

INTRODUCTION

Current instructional practices emphasize the integration of assessment and instruction, with the goal of educational practices that combine teaching with an on-going analysis of student progress towards instructional goals (Airasian, 1991). In spite of the importance of assessment, many teachers are often involved in assessment-related decision-making processes without having enough background or training in assessment (Popham, 2009; DeLuca, 2012; Lam, 2015; Mede & Atay, 2017). As a consequence, according to Stiggins (2010), "assessment illiteracy abounds" (p. 233). Teachers are found not to be able to judge the quality of their own assessment tasks (Bol & Strage, 1996). The fact that teachers' assessment strategies and practices are affected by their beliefs about the purpose and nature of assessment seems obvious (Brown, 2009; Delandshere & Jones, 1999). Through discussions about what is meant by assessment literacies, we can open up our practices to develop shared understandings rather than assuming that we share common needs and knowledge.

The extent of how well teachers, policy officers, teacher educators, researchers and professional bodies support the development of teacher assessment literacies can be measured by the development of assessment literacies. Developing teacher assessment literacy should be part of the ethical and moral responsibility to provide opportunity for all students to receive quality education. Despite the importance of assessment in education, most research in Turkey on finding out teachers' beliefs about teaching methodologies, skills, learning theories (Borg, 2003, 2018; Phipps & Borg, 2009) and there is little focus on the beliefs of teachers' on assessment. Thus, in the present study our aim was to compare the assessment literacy levels of two groups of teachers: teachers who are entitled with formal assessment roles and responsibilities and teachers without any specific formal assessment roles and responsibilities in Turkey at a private universities preparatory school.

It would be important to compare if teachers' beliefs change by taking on responsibilities on assessment. Since there is limited training on assessment and most teachers who do not have had any roles in the area of assessment are not

© KONINKLIJKE BRILL NV, LEIDEN, 2019 | DOI:10.1163/9789004393455_007 equipped with preparing tests, providing feedback and using assessment as tool to boost student learning (Mede & Atay, 2017) which are a core area in ensuring quality in language education. It might be crucial to put more emphasis on researching two different groups of teachers' conceptions on this area and make suggestions regarding teacher education and teacher training programmes as part of professional development in Turkey.

LITERATURE REVIEW

Teacher Assessment Literacy

Chappuis, Stiggins, Chappuis, and Arter (2012) define classroom assessment literacy as necessary knowledge and skill for compiling data about students' achievement and for effectively utilizing the assessment process and the assessment to enhance students' achievement. Assessment is an integral part of instruction, and effective instruction cannot take place without good assessment of students. Studies have indicated that when teachers integrate their assessment knowledge with their instruction, students benefit a lot in terms of academic success, metacognitive functions, and motivation for learning (Black & William, 1998; Gardner, 2006; Willis, 2010).

There are three goals of the educational assessment of students and teachers need to be clearly informed about these: assessment *for* learning, assessment *of* learning and assessing *as* learning (Earl, 2005). Assessment for learning refers to formative assessment conducted by teachers who regularly monitor the progress of students based on learning objectives (Stiggins, 2005). Teachers can scaffold students' learning through ongoing provision of feedback by regarding the strength and weakness of each. In this type of assessment, elicited evidence is used by teacher to adjust their ongoing instructional activities, or by students to adjust the ways they are trying to learn something. Assessing of learning is used to accommodate what the students know and are able to perform. The outcomes of such assessment, in the form of marks or grades, reveal whether the instruction is successful as specified in the curriculum objectives. Finally, assessment as learning refers to type of assessment that places the emphasis on individual learning. Thus, assessment is conducted so as to enable the individuals to assess their own learning.

Lately, there has been a call for an increased emphasis on formative assessment designed to assist learning (William, 2011). Regarding this issue, William (2011) claim that "there is a strong body of theoretical and empirical work that suggests that integrating assessment with instruction may well have unprecedented power to increase student engagement and to improve learning outcomes" (p. 211). Therefore, pre-service and in-service teachers need to be aware of new trends in assessment which affect student learning. All in all, classroom assessment yields important data for teachers regarding students' learning; this data leads to further development and improvement of teachers' instruction and revision of curriculum content to better serve the students' needs, enabling them to learn efficiently and effectively (Qualters, 2001).

For quality assessment teachers need to meet the specific needs of learners, base the assessment on concrete and appropriate achievement goals, determine student achievement accurately, yield assessment outcomes that effectively communicate to users and involve student participation in self-assessment (DeLuca, 2012; Popham, 2013). One way to be able to achieve these is increasing a teacher's assessment literacy.

According to McMillan (2000), teachers who are well-informed about assessment literacy (AL hereafter) can integrate assessment with teaching in that way they can benefit from appropriate techniques of teaching. In that sense, teacher education programs and professional development experiences are thought to be important as they can provide teachers with current knowledge about learning and assessment, especially the knowledge and skills which are required to develop and improve assessment tasks that would elicit higher-order thinking skills of students or to assess their development and competence (Cizek, 2000). AL includes constructing dependable assessments and after that conduct and grade the assessments to facilitate valid instructional decisions (Popham, 2004; Stiggins, 2002). Fullan (2002) similarly claims that AL is inevitable for appraising teachers' understanding of their assessment procedures and assignments, and the quality of students' performance. Thus, because their impact on the education process can range from modest to major, classroom assessments ought to be as good as they can.

However, a brief examination of the literature on AL reveals findings with serious pedagogical implications. Despite repeated calls for enhanced teacher assessment literacy (Popham, 2013) research has continually demonstrated that teachers face significant challenges in integrating new approaches to assessment that align with contemporary mandates and assessment theories (Bennett, 2011). Many teachers feel prepared inadequately in assessment and feel that they need to get assistance in conducting different classroom assessments and in giving assessment-related decisions (Mertler, 1999; Mertler & Campbell, 2005). Many others maintain variable understandings about educational assessment leading to fundamentally different orientations and classroom practices. According to Fulcher (2012), "there are not many textbooks and learning materials available for non-specialists or those new to testing and assessment. Taylor (2009) also argued that most available textbooks are "highly technical or too specialized for language educators seeking to understand basic principles and practice in assessment" (p. 23).

Moreover, research also indicates limited pre-service assessment education in general (Galluzzo, 2005; Mertler, 2003). Preservice teachers in teacher education programs are rarely exposed to coursework or other experiences that teach them either about the role of assessment in learning or approaches to assessment that positively impact student learning (Stiggins, 2002). Across multiple studies, it is widely acknowledged that pre-service teachers typically enter teacher education programs with summative conceptions of assessment, rather than formative assessment concepts and their knowledge is based on their experiences with assessment as a student (Cowan, 2009).

Consequently, in pre-service education they take courses, though very few in number, which are expected to provide them with critical opportunities to develop knowledge in assessment theories and practical skills in the area. Gradually, pre-service teachers begin to shift their approaches to reflect more contemporary conceptions of assessment. To illustrate, collecting data from 69 teacher candidates in all four years of their concurrent programs within a large Canadian urban setting, Volante and Fazio (2007) found that most candidates favoured only summative assessment and lacked other forms of assessment knowledge and their levels of self-efficacy remained relatively low across each of the four years of program. To improve their assessment literacy, teacher candidates overwhelmingly endorsed the development of specific courses focusing on classroom assessment. In another study with pre-service teachers, Cowan (2009) found that formal assessment courses along with practicum experiences supported pre-service teachers' development of formative approaches to assessment. However, at the end of the four-year program, teachers were mainly using straightforward formative assessment practices, e.g. questioning, and rarely implementing more complex practices, e.g. self- and peer assessment. In a more recent study, Smith, Hill, Cowie, and Gilmore (2014) compared the assessment beliefs of first and third year pre-service teachers. Findings revealed that beliefs of pre-service teachers shifted from summative to more formative conceptualization at the end of the program; candidates became more aware of the role of students in the assessment process.

As a formal way of improving pre-service teacher AL, the quality of assessment courses has been of concern. Assessment courses are criticized for being theory laden and disconnected from teachers' classroom assessment practices. Thus, essential components for quality assessment courses, such as carefully-tailored content, well-trained instructors who can make connection between theory and practice, have been highly suggested (Jeong, 2013). However, many pre-service teacher education programs offer a one-semester assessment course that provides only a general introduction to assessment (Greenberg & Walsh, 2012). As current classroom assessment demands include the use of different assessment types for different purposes, developing teachers' comprehensive understandings across these elements is critical.

Similarly, research with in-service teachers reveals the need for continued support on assessment literacy in professional learning (Çalışkan & Kaşıkçı, 2010; Yamtim & Wongwanich, 2014). This support is said to be offered informally through classroom implementation and experimentation and through formal professional learning structures as many teachers are observed to be largely unprepared to effectively integrate assessment into their practice, with beginning teachers particularly lacking in confidence in this area (Mertler, 2004). Many in-service teachers report feeling ill-prepared to assess student learning and claim that their lack of preparation is largely due to inadequate pre-service training in educational measurement (Karaman & Şahin, 2014). On another note, Mede and Atay's (2017) study explored the assessment literacy of English teachers at preparatory schools at universities in

Turkey. The study showed that as teachers received limited education on assessment during pre-service education, there was an urgent need for an in-service training. The study also put forward practicing teachers' understanding of assessment and their ongoing training needs as a somewhat neglected area. Teacher AL training needs to become long-term, sustainable, individualized and on the job (Koh, 2011). Teachers' needs should be situated within the requirements of different educational contexts and trainings should be shaped according to the priorities of the educational context.

Teacher Beliefs on Assessment

Teachers' approaches to assessment are shaped by several factors including their previous experiences with assessment, as students and teachers, their values and beliefs on what constitutes valid and useful evidence of student learning, their knowledge of assessment theory, and the prevalence of systemic assessment policies (Popham, 2013). As Brown (2003) suggests teachers' beliefs regarding the process and purpose of assessment and the nature of teacher and learning have influences on all pedagogical acts. According to Brown (2002, 2003), teachers hold one of the four conceptions related to assessment: (a) it is useful because it can provide information for improving instruction; (b) it is necessary for making students accountable; (c) it is necessary for making institutions accountable; and (d) it is irrelevant to teaching and learning.

According to Munoz, Palacio and Escobar (2012), when assessment practices rely on teachers' beliefs, identifying those beliefs to reach a common understanding of assessment and observing whether there are disagreements between teachers and other decision makers. Some studies (Rueda & Garcia, 1994; Delandshere & Jones, 1996; Brown, 2003) have indicated that teachers' beliefs about assessment and how those beliefs shape their classroom practice should be revealed as different beliefs may lead to different assessment practices. Woods (1996) studied on teachers' beliefs and suggested some methods like logs, video-based recall, lesson plans, and interview questions. These methods help teachers to reveal their previous teaching and language-learning experiences and their influence on their present views and practices (p. 27).

Brown (2002) has recommended a different method to study teacher beliefs. He developed a Teacher's Conceptions of Assessment (TCOA) inventory which will also be used in this study as well. According to TCOA, four purposes were enough to comprehend teachers' beliefs about the aim of assessment. These aims were: (a) assessment improves teaching and learning; (b) assessment is about certification of students' learning; (c) assessment demonstrates the quality of schools; and (d) assessment is irrelevant to the work of teacher and students' learning.

Brown's conception tries to reveal that thanks to assessment students can be informed about the progress of their learning process, and also the quality of teaching (Black & Wiliam, 1998; Crooks, 1988). The second conception is about students' performance in exams to enter in high levels of education or to graduate. The third one is related to the uses of assessment to prove schools' and teachers' ability to provide quality education. Finally, the fourth conception is related to assessment being irrelevant. This is based on the assumption that teachers know the curriculum and their students, so there is no need to conduct formal assessment.

To sum up, understanding teacher beliefs on assessment is important to provide a better education and to increase student learning. This can be done by using different methods which will eventually produce data from different contexts.

Turkish Preparation Schools & Teacher Background

According to a recent survey conducted by British Council (Guven et al., 2015), there is a rapid increase in the number of universities in the last 15 years. According to the report "English is traditionally taught at Turkish universities in a one-year preparatory school teaching 'foundation', 'basic' or 'access' English, and then through language support classes during undergraduate programmes" (p. 69). While the first preparation school was at Bogazici University in 1958, it was followed by Middle East Technical University in 1960s, in 1996 all English-Medium Universities had preparation schools and since 2002 a preparation school has become a must in all Turkish universities.

The high increase in preparation schools created a need for high number of language instructors in a short amount time. The result of this increase created issues in teacher education as many instructors were hired by the universities and new curriculum and assessment systems were needed. Since most preparatory schools prepared students for EMI, the exit assessment system and all assessment systems in the programmes became hugely important.

In fact, it has been recommended that there is a need for valid and reliable assessment mechanisms. In order to have more valid & reliable assessment tools and evaluation, there is apparently a need for more teacher awareness and education in this specific area. A valid concern has been raised related to assessment at preparatory programmes in the report. The "concern is how levels are assessed. In some cases, international examinations are used for the exit proficiency test, either IELTS or institutional TOEFL. In all other cases in-house tests are used and the quality of these is extremely variable: some universities have invested heavily in training members of their testing units but others seem to be much less professional" (p. 77). According to the report, new policies are required to increase quality in terms of valid assessment. Also, the training needs and teacher promotions need to be done according to contextual needs and qualifications.

Another important national report published by British Council in cooperation with TEPAV project team called "Turkey National Needs Assessment of State School English Language Teaching" (Vale, 2013). The report recommends that teacher development and training sessions on assessment need to take place since contemporary assessment methods such as continuous assessment, portfolio assessment or self/peer assessment methods are integrated into the assessment system, yet "there is little relevant guidance within the Student or Teacher books to say how such processes may be taken forward" (p. 57).

Based on the needs assessment reports, it could be concluded that there needs to be some special training for understanding assessment of English at schools and some expertise is required. Since not all schools give much importance to assessment or its training, only teachers with special interest in this area, or the ones who receive training on assessment take up the roles and promoted. The rest of the school and the system relies on these teachers' knowledge and expertise.

METHODOLOGY

Significance of the Study

It is important to understand the attitudes or beliefs of teachers in a specific school context in order to bring changes to the existing system, to further dig into specific areas for improvement and to make new policies. In addition, understanding teachers' common beliefs about assessment may be a good start for continuing professional development and for the provision of high quality and fair language education and assessment. If undertaking responsibilities and going through training on assessment in a school creates a difference or a positive change in teachers' beliefs, it is important to understand further what the reasons are for this difference and how they can be used beneficially for improved teaching and learning purposes and more standard and high quality education provision.

For these reasons, it is important to conduct this preliminary research comparing the responses of teachers with assessment responsibilities and training vs. teachers without any assessment responsibilities to see the worth in investing teacher education in assessment. Besides, based on the literature review on this, there is little study conducted to understand the assessment perceptions of English language teachers in general. There is also little research conducted in Turkish context, especially at higher education. Besides, there is a call for more fair and valid assessment system and training on assessment. For these reasons, this study will fill this gap in related literature and provide justifications and evidence for school-wide assessment training needs.

Research Questions

The goal of this study was to identify the concepts of assessment held by language teachers working in Turkish higher education preparatory school context. It also aimed to find if there was a statistically significant difference in the attitudes of teachers who have held positions or responsibilities and received training in assessment unit of a university in addition to their teaching responsibility and who have only teaching responsibility. Thus, this study aims at answering the following research questions:

1. What are the Turkish language teachers' perceptions of assessment working at a university's preparatory school?
2. Is there a statistically significant difference in terms of understanding of assessment concepts between English teachers who are entitled with formal

assessment roles and responsibilities and teachers who are not entitled with such roles and responsibilities within an institution?

Data Collection Tools & Analysis Methods

This study involved a self-report attitude inventory (TCoA-III) taken from Brown (2004). There were 27 items with closed-ended rating scales (Likert's 6-point scale) and one open-ended opinion question which provided the qualitative data. This is a descriptive study with quantitative and qualitative data. The quantitative data helps to understand the beliefs and qualitative data helps to further elicit and interpret the outstanding points arising from the quantitative data.

The items in the survey express an opinion from four main purposes of assessment. These four main purposes include assessment of learning and teaching, school accountability, student accountability, and treating assessment as irrelevant. Brown (2002) designed and evaluated two different versions of the self-reported attitude inventory and used it with two different participant groups and excluded ill-fitting items to the model for validity and reliability purposes. "After two rounds of data analysis, a multi-factorial, two-level, inter-correlated model of teachers' conceptions of assessment was developed in which the statements created nine conceptions of assessment, seven of which load onto two higher-order factors" (Brown, 2004, p. 308). In the end COA-III was created and this research, the latest version was used.

In this study, since the participants are all competent English language teachers and students are not included in this study, the questionnaire was administered in English, in the original language. All the assessment related terms are familiar to the participants since they have teaching qualifications, so we didn't want to cause any confusions in translating the questionnaire in a different language as this would risk the reliability of the questionnaire.

During the analysis stage, for demographic information, descriptive statistics by means of SPSS was used. For inferential statistics, both parametric (t-test) and non-parametric (Mann-U Whitney) tests were used. All normality tests were analyzed and the most suitable tests to compare the means of two groups were chosen. More detailed information is given below about the analysis results and procedures.

For qualitative data analysis, participants' answers of open-ended questions were coded and themes and sub-themes are drawn. To ensure the reliability of analysis, two coders were used and similar results are reported.

Research Context & Participants

The study took place in an English medium university preparation school in Turkey. Only the volunteer teachers in the institution responded to the questionnaire although the questionnaire was given to all teachers working at the school. The participants randomly included teachers who have been entitled with an assessment responsibility and roles in the current institution or in the previous institutions and the teachers who have never held any assessment related roles and responsibilities. We didn't want to limit the study to the teachers who have had roles only in the current institution since the opinions of most teachers might have been changed by the previous assessment responsibilities held in other institutions. In the current institution, when a teacher is given a role or a responsibility, this role entails teaching students in reduced hours (between 4 hrs to 10 hours) in order to create time to fulfil the given responsibilities and preparing quizzes or exams according to the curriculum and student needs, as well as conducting assessment related standardization sessions. If the teachers are not asked to take any assessment related responsibilities, they are asked to purely design lessons and teach. They are only involved in administering and marking exams and quizzes as far as assessment responsibility is concerned. The summary of the demographic information with frequencies (F) and percentages (%) are shown in Table 7.1.

As shown in Table 7.1, the data consisted of 33 participants (n=33), of which 72.7 % (n=24) was female. This reflects the nature of the population in Turkey. The majority of the teachers in the sample data can be considered as experienced teachers as only 9.1 % (n=3) of the participants said that they have had 1 to 5 years of teaching experience. The rest has above 5 years of teaching experience. Twenty-one teachers (63.3%) said that they have had assessment training. Their explanations to the nature of trainings included assessment related 2 or 3-day one-shot training workshops with a trainer. They also reported that they had received courses as part of their BA and MA studies. Twenty participants in the group stated that they have been given assessment related roles and responsibilities. While 17 of these teachers have had an assessment training, 3 of them conducted their responsibilities without a specialized training on assessment. Thirteen teachers in the sample group said that they have never had any assessment related responsibilities or been given specific roles in assessment.

Table 7.1. Demographic information on study participants

Gender			Qualifications			Assessment training			Years of teaching experience			Assessment role		
	F	%		F	%		F	%		F	%		F	%
Female	24	72.7	Only MA	15	45.4	YES	21	63.6	1 to 5 Years	3	9.1	YES	20	60.6
Male	9	27.3	PhD	4	12.2	NO	12	36.4	6 to 10 Years	17	51.5	NO	13	39.4
			MA&CELTA	6	18.2				11 and more	13	39.4			
			MA&DELTA	8	24.2									

FINDINGS

Findings of the Quantitative Data

As mentioned in the previous part, Concepts of Assessment IIIA scale in Brown and Remesal's study (2012) uses 27 statements and they are distributed equally across nine different factors. The factors are organised into 4 major concepts or purposes. Table 7.2 shows all participating teachers' concepts of assessment in one school according to 9 factors. Table 7.3 also reports the concepts of assessment according to obtaining a formal role in assessment or not. This way it is possible to get an overview of the teachers' concepts of assessment in comparison.

Table 7.2 shows the overall views of all teachers according to the factors identified by the questionnaire. According to the responses, most of the participants in the sample group believe that assessment contributes to student learning and most disagree that assessment does not have negative washback effect. These two results support each other. Only few teachers with a mean of 2.61 believe that assessment results are ignored. These all show that assessment has a big place and teachers give importance to assessment. They mostly agree that it also improves instruction in general and assessment is seen as a contributing factor. Teachers are doubtful with a mean of 3.72 about the feedback gained from assessment about student success (assessment provides imprecise information). They also do not strongly believe (mean score 3.49) that the institution and the teachers are hold accountable regarding assessment results. Assessment neither reflects schools' success nor teachers' own success.

Table 7.2. Descriptive statistics for the COA of all teachers (n=33)

Factors	Min.	Max.	M	SD
Assessment describes student performance	3	5.3	4.48	0.60
Assessment improves student learning	4	6	4.96	0.59
Assessment improves instruction	3.33	6	4.59	0.70
Assessment info is valid	3	5.67	4.13	0.62
Assessment results are ignored	1	5	2.61	0.83
Assessment makes students accountable	3	5.33	4.29	0.70
Assessment makes schools (and teachers) accountable	2	5	3.49	0.76
Assessment provides imprecise information (in accurate)	2.33	5.33	3.72	0.69
Assessment has negative washback effects (bad)	1.33	4.67	2.84	0.86

Table 7.3 shows the responses of two different groups of teachers which gives the opportunity to compare the opinions of both groups. In order to find out if there is a significant difference in 9 factors in assessment, the mean scores of the two groups of teachers were compared by using a parametric test; independent *t-test* and a non-parametric test; *Mann-Whitney U* test.

Table 7.3. Descriptive statistics for the COA of teachers with and without an assessment role

Factors	With a role (n=20)				Without a role (n=13)			
	Min.	Max.	M	SD	Min.	Max.	M	SD
Assessment describes student performance	3	5.3	4.49	0.63	3.3	5.3	4.49	0.60
Assessment improves student learning	4.33	6	5.08	0.55	4	6	4.79	0.63
Assessment improves instruction	3.67	6	4.67	0.72	3.33	5.67	4.49	0.69
Assessment info is valid	3	5.67	4.23	0.64	3	5.33	3.97	0.58
Assessment results are ignored	1	5	2.6	0.90	1.67	4	2.71	0.75
Assessment makes students accountable	3	5.33	4.25	0.73	3.33	5.33	4.3	0.66
Assessment makes schools (and teachers) accountable	2.33	5	3.5	0.68	2	5	3.4	0.89
Assessment provides imprecise information (in accurate)	2.33	5.33	3.7	0.74	2.33	4.67	3.77	0.65
Assessment has negative washback effects (bad)	1.33	4.67	2.7	0.82	1.67	4.33	3	0.93

To determine if the sample population of each group showed normal distribution to run a parametric test, Skewness and Kurtosis values for each factor and for both groups were checked. The data for two groups (teachers with an assessment role and teachers without an assessment role), for each factor were a little skewed and kurtotic, but they didn't differ significantly from normality. The assumption was that the data were approximately normally distributed, in terms of skewness and kurtosis. When, Shapiro-Wilk test results were checked for each factor, 2 factors (Assessment improves student learning and assessment makes students accountable) did not show normal distribution. Therefore, it was possible to compute independent T-test for 7 factors. For the other 2 factors, Mann-Whitney U test, a non-parametric test, was used to compare the means of the sample groups. *P* value for both tests were set as 0.05. This provided a 95% confidence level.

An independent T-test assumes that the variances are equal. In order to understand this, Levene's test scores were checked for the seven factors which showed normal distribution. Three of the seven factors (assessment is valid; assessment has negative backwash effect – it is bad; assessment makes schools accountable) didn't show equal variance, therefore they were also excluded from this parametric test (independent t-test).

The results of the independent t-test for 4 factors did not show any significant difference between two groups of teachers with P values 0.974 > 0.05 for assessment defines student performance; *p* value .484 > .05 for assessment improves instruction. factor that is "assessment improves instruction" showed significant difference with a *p* value 0.484 > 0.05.

Mann-Whitney U test was computed for factors which were non-normally distributed and for the three factors which didn't show equal variances in Levene's test values. Similarly, there wasn't a significant difference between the two groups of teachers as all P values were greater than 0.05.

Although there wasn't a statistically significant difference between two groups, in some factors, mean averages of the given responses to the 6-point Likert scale, showed slight differences. According to the descriptive statistics in Tables 7.2 and 7.3, all the teachers clearly agree that assessment improves students learning and it has a positive impact on their success. However, the results showed that teacher with an assessment role tended to disagree that the assessment is bad and has negative backwash effect to teaching and learning compared to teachers with no assessment. This shows that they have stronger belief in the usefulness of the exams in general. This feeling might come from various reasons. They might have created ownership to the role and their beliefs might have turned positive or they might have seen the positive sides over the years by experience.

They also believe in the validity of the exams. While teachers with no assessment role, has weaker feelings towards the validity issue of the exams. One area that teachers believe is the inaccuracy of the exams. They believe that exams may not reflect real student performance. In fact, this finding is in line with the validity and the negative effect factors. Teachers who believe exams are imprecise in their nature, also think that they may not be valid and may have negative effects. Teacher with an assessment role believe that assessment increases school accountability. They might again feel this way because of the give responsibility in because they are responsible for the development of the exams.

Findings of Qualitative Data

Of the 33 participants, 23 provided an answer for this open-ended and optional question. This means the response rate for the question was 70%. Besides, most of the participants provided more than the question asked from them. To analyze these 23 responses, a bottom-up inductive approach was adopted and the process was data-driven. The data were read and re-read, coded and recoded, and the accounts were organized in themes. The resulting frame exposed 3 main categories and 7 main themes and 6 sub-themes. The names and brief definitions of the themes are presented in Table 7.4.

As Table 7.4 suggests, the first theme "Change" was the prevalent theme. There were 15 accounts identified in this theme. A significant number of participants expressed their perception of assessment as one that would provide them development in their teaching practices "Raising awareness", "becoming more effective", "shaping future plans and teaching practices" are example accounts that fall into this theme category.

Table 7.4. Themes regarding teacher perceptions of assessment that emerge from the written responses of the participants

Themes and sub-themes	Definition

1. Change in teacher development
   1.1. Discovery
   1.2. Transformation
   1.3. Growth
   1.4. Improvement
   1.5. Awareness
	Gaining new perspectives about their teaching, changing completely, moving from simple to more complex and advanced, becoming better and more effective in reflection, or recognizing what is happening around and and shaping their future career according to their experiences in assessment, being more aware with student success by empathising them.

2. Material Development	Becoming more aware of material choice, material preparation and material adaptation. Better materials.
3. Achievable Objectives	

4. Nature of Assessment
   4.1. Quality
   4.2. Valid
   4.3. Reliable
   4.4. Process-oriented
   4.5. Realistic
   4.6. Objective
   4.7. Meaningful	

5. Change in student attitudes
   5.1. Discovery
   5.2. Awareness
   5.2. Improvement
	Reflecting on their own learning process, being aware of their weaknesses and strengths, contributing to their study skills.

DISCUSSION

One aspect of becoming an effective teacher is developing *assessment literacy*, or the ability to develop assessments that transform the learning goals into assessment activities that accurately reflect student understanding and achievement (Mertler & Campbell, 2005). This study is unique in that it examines and compares the views of teachers who are entitled with formal assessment roles and responsibilities and who are not entitled with such specific roles and responsibilities. Overall, this study shows one significant fact that regardless of being entitled as an "assessor", *all* teachers need to possess some degree of AL and participate in assessment related roles actively. Especially, when the *three* goals of assessment (Earl, 2005) are considered to be contributing factors to students learning, all teachers need to be capable of utilizing different assessment methods.

While the teachers who are entitled with assessment roles are more into preparing and managing summative forms of assessment types, all teachers need to have knowledge about formative assessment tools or in-class assessment methods as they are the contemporary methods which are used and required by most schools and policy makers. For more effective on-going in-class assessment methods and quality instruction, not only teachers with assessment roles, but all teachers can be asked to participate in teacher development programmes and session which focus on assessment. AL seems to be an integral part of professional development.

More specifically, the findings of the qualitative data showed that teachers entitled with assessment roles and responsibilities at their institution agree that assessment literacy contributes to their professional development to a greater extend. Most of them stated that they have gained new perspectives in teaching and also in life. They said that they have learned to put themselves in students' positions which helped them to acquire some complex thinking skills. In addition to this, they indicated that they become more effective and better educators by assessing students' performances. This change and awareness help them shape their future careers in teaching. In that sense these findings is in line with what Stiggins (1991a) suggested which was giving the value to the assessment to reach clear, specific and rich definitions of the student achievement. Assessment literates are also aware of the fact this theoretical knowledge help them develop better materials. They suggested that they can choose better materials, and adapt those materials according to the needs of their students.

Another theme emerged from the open-ended survey question is that thanks to assessment literacy, teachers can set achievable goals as they are more aware of the realities of their students. They can know what their students can or cannot do. They do not go after the ideal and push students, but they try to attain high performances. In this respect, this finding is also in line with the related literature (Black & Wiliam, 1998; Gardner, 2006; Willis, 2010) which puts forward the importance of integration of assessment to the teaching in terms of students' academic success, metacognitive functions, and motivation for learning. Assessment literate teachers were in consensus about the nature of the assessment. They think that assessment should be quality, valid, reliable, process-oriented, realistic, objective and meaningful.

This finding emphasize the importance of teacher beliefs which can affect their classroom practices. This issue was largely mentioned in the related literature (Brown, 2002 & 2003; Johnson, 1994; Delandshere & Jones, 1996; Rueda & Garcia, 1994). The last theme emerged from teachers' answers was about how assessment change students' behaviours. They asserted that if assessment results are shared with students, they can have clear ideas about their own learning progress and become more aware of their weaknesses and strengths which can help them acquire some study skills.

With regards to quantitative results, all the data was mostly normally distributed in the study and there wasn't a big standard deviation in the results; therefore, it is possible to generalize the findings to a larger group. The opinions of the teachers responding to the prompts were mostly homogenous which makes it stronger to conclude that the results are likely to reflect the views of a larger population.

In some school structures, exams are prepared by a limited number of teachers specialized in this area receiving specific training. Results show that people with assessment roles and responsibilities might have more positive beliefs about their validity and accountability. This might suggest that if the roles are given to all teachers if teachers feel accountable and receive some in-service training on exam preparation and participate in the design of exams, their beliefs might change.

Both quantitative and qualitative findings might indicate that for teachers, assessment reliability and validity carry importance. This might also shape their beliefs in both negative and positive ways. Also, as the literature reveals, if teachers become good assessors, their students' success may increase as they gain more awareness into learning objectives and feel accountable.

According to the results of the quantitative and qualitative findings, exams are very important; they affect instruction, and student learning. This may show the exam-oriented nature of teachers, programmes and the students. However, teachers do not want to be accountable for the exam results. This is also somewhat interesting and needs further exploration. Most teachers raised their concerns towards validity and the reliability of the exams. Perhaps, they may think that the results do not reflect the accurate performance that's why no one wants to feel accountable. However, teacher with no roles feel more strongly about this issue. Therefore it is possible to conclude that if someone is responsible in the design of the assessment tools, they may feel more positive about the exam tools and process' validity and accountability.

This brings another issue: exam preparation and better teacher development in the assessment. Teachers, especially who design assessment tools need to be well equipped. As the British council reports (2013, 2015) suggest better assessment tools are needed and one way to achieve this is training teachers an investing more in this area. Assessment, instruction, and teacher development are the three important areas which make a system effective and successful, so none of them should be ignored or neglected.

CONCLUSION

The present study investigates the attitudes of Turkish teachers towards assessment. It aims to also compare two groups of teachers to find out if the concepts of assessment change as a result of taking up a responsibility in assessment in an institution. The results of qualitative and quantitative findings indicate that although teachers' concepts do not change significantly, teachers with assessment responsibilities have a more positive attitude towards some purposes of assessment such as its usefulness and accuracy and school accountability. Yet, both groups believe that assessment positively contributes to students learning and impacts instruction.

It is also clear from the qualitative data that validity of an exam is crucial. Teachers state that they gain better understanding towards learning, teaching and students' needs with the help of their assessment experience that comes with their role. In addition, this study revealed that teacher assessment literacy contributes not only to teacher development but also student development.

This was a small-scale study which aimed at providing some insight into English language teachers' perceptions of assessment literacy. Because of the busy schedule, only one open-ended question was involved to the study. For future studies, the researcher(s) can interview with the teachers to gain more information. The next limitation is about the participants. There were only 33 participants in the study, there could have been more teachers which would have made it possible to conduct factor analysis to find the emerging concepts more accurately, and also maybe teachers from different institutions could have been involved in the study. Their ideas, beliefs, emotions and their academic background related to AL might have been questioned and also the mismatches of their beliefs may have been revealed. Besides, student views are also important in a teaching and learning environment. Therefore, a similar questionnaire might also be given to gain student aspect. To keep all of these in mind, this study is preliminary and gives a general idea about the topic. To identify if there is a significant change in any of the factors, more participants are needed or an in-depth focused group discussion and interviews are needed. Besides, teachers' views about the necessity of AL and training can be investigated for further studies.

REFERENCES

Airasian, P. W. (1991). Perspectives on measurement instruction. *Educational Measurement: Issues and Practice, 10*(1), 13–16, 26.

Bennett, R. E. (2011). Formative assessment: A critical review. *Assessment in Education: Principles & Policy & Practice, 18*(1), 5–25.

Black, P., & William, D. (1998). *Inside the black box: Raising standards through classroom assessment.* London: Granada Learning.

Bol, L., & Strage, A. (1996). The contradiction between teachers' instructional goals and their assessment practices in high school biology courses. *Science Education, 80,* 145–163.

Brown, G. T. L. (2002). *Teachers' conceptions of assessment* (Unpublished doctoral dissertation). University of Auckland, Auckland, New Zealand.

Brown, G. T. L. (2003). *Teachers' instructional conceptions: Assessment's relationship to learning, teaching, curriculum, and teacher efficacy.* Paper presented at the Joint Conference of the Australian and New Zealand Associations for Research in Education, Auckland, New Zealand.

Brown, G. T. L. (2004). Teachers' conceptions of assessment: Implications for policy and professional development. *Assessment in Education, 11*(3), 301–318.

Brown, G. T. L. (2009). Teachers' self-reported assessment practices and conceptions: Using structural equation modelling to examine measurement and structural models. In T. Teo & M. S. Khine (Eds.), *Structural equation modelling in educational research: Concepts and applications* (pp. 243–266). Rotterdam, The Netherlands: Sense Publishers.

Brown, G. T. L., & Remesal, A. (2012). Prospective teachers' conceptions of assessment: A cross-cultural comparison. *The Spanish Journal of Psychology, 15*(1), 75–89.

Borg, S. (2003). Teacher cognition in language teaching: A review of research on what language learners think, know, believe, and do. *Language Teaching, 36*(2), 81–109.

Borg, S. (2018). Teachers' beliefs and classroom practices. In P. Garrett & J. M. Cots (Eds.), *The Routledge handbook of language awareness* (pp. 75–91). London: Routledge.

Çalışkan, H., & Kaşıkçı, Y. (2010). The application of traditional and alternative assessment and evaluation tools by teachers in social studies. *Procedia Social and Behavioral Sciences, 2,* 4152–4156.

Chappuis, J., Stiggins, R., Chappuis, S., & Arter, J. (2012). *Classroom assessment for student learning: Doing it right-using it well.* Portland, RA: Assessment Training Institute.

Cizek, G. J. (2000). Pockets of resistance in the assessment revolution. *Educational Measurement: Issues and Practice, 19*(2), 16–23.

Cowan, E. M. (2009). Implementing formative assessment: Student teachers' experiences on placements. *Teacher Development, 13*(1), 71–84.

Crooks, T. (1988). The impact of classroom evaluation practices on students. *Review of Educational Research, 58*(4), 438–481.

Delandshere, G., & Jones, J. H. (1999). Elementary teachers' beliefs about assessment in mathematics: A case of assessment paralysis. *Journal of Curriculum and Supervision, 14*(3), 216–240.

DeLuca, C. (2012). Preparing teachers for the age of accountability: Toward a framework for assessment education. *Teacher Education Yearbook XXI: A Special Issue of Action in Teacher Education, 34*(5–6), 576–591.

Earl, L. (2005). *Thinking about purpose in classroom assessment: Assessment for, as and of learning.* Manitoba: Australian Curriculum Studies Association.

Fulcher, G. (2012) Assessment literacy for the language classroom. *Language Assessment Quarterly, 9*(2), 113–132.

Fullan, M. (2002). The role of leadership in the promotion of knowledge management in schools. *Teacher and Teaching: Theory and Practice, 8*(3), 409–419.

Galluzzo, G. R. (2005). Performance assessment and renewing teacher education the possibilities of the NBPTS standards. *The Clearing House: A Journal of Educational Strategies, Issues and Ideas, 78*(4), 142–145. doi:10.3200/TCHS.78.4.142-145

Gardner, J. (2006). Assessment for learning: A compelling conceptualization. In J. Gardner (Ed.), *Assessment and learning* (pp. 197–204). London: Sage Publications.

Greenberg, J., & Walsh, K. (2012). *What teacher preparation programs teach about K-12 assessment: A review.* Washington, DC: National Council on Teacher Quality.

Guven, A., Parry, J., & Ergenekon, T. (2015). *The state of English in higher education in Turkey: The baseline study.* Ankara: British Council. Retrieved from https://www.britishcouncil.org.tr/sites/default/files/he_baseline_study_book_web_-_son.pdf

Jeong, H. (2013). Defining assessment literacy: Is it different for language testers and non-language testers? *Language Testing, 30*(3), 345–362.

Johnson, K. E. (1994). The emerging beliefs and instructional practices of preservice English as-a-second-language teachers. *Teacher and Teacher Education, 10*(4), 439–452.

Karaman, P., & Şahin, Ç. (2014). Investigating the assessment literacy of teacher candidates. *Ahi Evran Üniversitesi Kırşehir Eğitim Fakültesi Dergisi (KEFAD), 15*(2), 175–189.

Koh, K. H. (2011). Improving teachers' assessment literacy through professional development. *Teaching Education, 22*(3), 255–276.

Lam, R. (2015). Language assessment training in Hong Kong: Implications for language assessment literacy. *Language Testing, 32*(2), 169–197.

McMillan, J. H. (2000). Fundamental assessment principles for teachers and school administrators. *Practical Assessment, Research and Evaluation, 7*(8), 1–9.

Mede, E., & Atay, D. (2017). English language teachers' assessment literacy: The Turkish context. *Dil Dergisi, 168*(1), 43–60.

Mertler, C. A. (1999). Assessing student performance: A descriptive study of the classroom assessment practices of Ohio teachers. *Education, 120*, 285–296.

Mertler, C. A. (2003, October 15–18). *Preservice versus inservice teachers' assessment literacy: Does classroom experience make a difference?* The Annual Meeting of the Mid-Western Educational Research Association, Columbus, OH.

Mertler, C. A. (2004). Secondary teachers' assessment literacy: Does classroom experience make a difference? *American Secondary Education, 33*(1), 49–64.

Mertler, C. A., & Campbell, C. (2005). *Measuring teachers' knowledge & application of classroom assessment concepts: Development of the assessment literacy inventory.* Paper presented at the annual meeting of the American Educational Research Association, Montreal, Quebec, Canada.

Muñoz, A. P., Palacio, M., & Escobar, L. (2012). Teachers' beliefs about assessment in an EFL context in Colombia. *Profile: Issues in Teachers' Professional Development, 14*(1), 143–156.

National Institute of Education. (2009). *A teacher education model for the 21st century.* Singapore: Author.

Phipps, S., & Borg, S. (2009). Exploring tensions between teachers' grammar teaching beliefs and practices. *System, 37,* 380–390.

Popham, W. J. (2004). Why assessment illiteracy is professional suicide. *Educational Leadership, 62,* 82–82.

Popham, W. J. (2009). Assessment literacy for teachers: Faddish or fundamental? *Theory into Practice, 48*(1), 4–11.

Popham, W. J. (2013). *Classroom assessment: What teachers need to know* (7th ed.). Boston, MA: Pearson.

Qualters, D. M. (2001). *Using classroom assessment data to improve student learning* (Classroom assessment guidebook). Boston, MA: Northeastern University. Retrieved from http://www.northeastern.edu/cietl/wp-content/uploads/2012/02/assessment_nu.pdf

Rueda, R., & Garcia, E. (1994). *Teachers' beliefs about reading assessment with Latino language minority students* (Center for research on education, diversity & excellence, NCRCDSLL research reports). Berkeley, CA: University of California.

Smith, L. F., Hill, M. F., Cowie, B., & Gilmore, A. (2014). Preparing teachers to use the enabling power of assessment. In C. Wyatt-Smith, V. Klenowski, & P. Colbert (Eds.), *Designing assessment for quality learning* (pp. 303–323). Dordrecht: Springer.

Stiggins, R. J. (1991). Assessment literacy. *Phi Delta Kappan, 72,* 534–539.

Stiggins, R. J. (2002). Assessment crisis: The absence of assessment for learning. *Phi Delta Kappan, 83,* 758–765.

Stiggins, R. J. (2010). Essential formative assessment competencies for teachers and school leaders. In H. L. Andrade & G. J. Cizek (Eds.), *Handbook of formative assessment* (pp. 233–250). New York, NY: Taylor & Francis.

Taylor, L. (2009). Developing assessment literacy. *Annual Review of Applied Linguistics, 29,* 21–36.

Vale, D. (2013). *Turkey National needs assessment of state school english language teaching.* Ankara: British Council & TAPEV. Retrieved from https://www.britishcouncil.org.tr/sites/default/files/turkey_national_needs_assessment_of_state_school_english_language_teaching.pdf

Volante, L., & Fazio, X. (2007). Exploring teacher candidates' assessment literacy: Implications for teacher education reform and professional development. *Canadian Journal of Education, 30*(3), 749–770.

Wiliam, D. (2011). What is assessment for learning? *Studies in Educational Evaluation, 37*(1), 3–14.

Willis, J. (2010). Assessment for learning as a participatory pedagogy. *Assessment Matters, 2,* 65–84.

Woods, D. (1996). *Teacher cognition in language teaching.* Cambridge: Cambridge University Press.

Yamtim, V., & Wongwanich, S. (2014). A study of classroom assessment literacy of primary school teachers. *Procedia – Social and Behavioral Sciences, 116,* 2998–3004.

Bahar Hasirci
Ozyegin University Istanbul
Turkey

Didem Karakuzular
Istanbul Medipol University Istanbul
Turkey

Derin Atay Bahçeşehir
University Istanbul
Turkey

Printed in the United States
By Bookmasters